The Festive Flavors of New Year

The Festive Flavors of New Year

Matthew Petchinsky

The Festive Flavors of New Year: A Culinary Celebration

By: Matthew Petchinsky

Introduction: Welcome to a New Year's Culinary Journey

As the clock strikes midnight and a new year begins, we gather with family, friends, and loved ones to celebrate the promise of new beginnings. The New Year is more than just a transition on the calendar; it's a celebration of life, hope, and unity. And what better way to usher in this fresh chapter than with a table full of vibrant dishes, steeped in tradition and brimming with flavors from around the world?

This cookbook, *The Festive Flavors of New Year: A Culinary Celebration*, is your guide to crafting memorable feasts that embody the spirit of renewal and joy. It's a culinary journey that embraces the rich diversity of global traditions while inviting you to create your own customs that resonate with your heart and home.

The Power of Food in New Year's Celebrations

Food has always been central to New Year's celebrations across cultures. Whether it's a symbolic dish representing prosperity, a comforting meal shared with loved ones, or a delectable treat enjoyed in solitude as a moment of self-care, food is a universal language of celebration. Every bite carries meaning, from the round fruits of the Philippines that signify good fortune to the long noodles of Japan that symbolize longevity. In this book, you'll find recipes inspired by these traditions and more, each infused with the essence of celebration.

A Culinary Journey Around the World

As you turn the pages, you'll discover how different cultures mark the New Year through food. Travel to Italy, where lentils and sausages promise abundance, or to Spain, where the tradition of eating 12 grapes at midnight ensures good luck for each month ahead. Visit the American South for black-eyed peas and cornbread, symbolizing wealth and health, or savor the tangy and spicy dishes of India, where vibrant flavors set the tone for an equally colorful year.

This book doesn't just stop at tradition—it encourages you to experiment and blend these global inspirations with your unique culinary flair. From plant-based delights to indulgent roasts, every recipe is designed to bring people together and celebrate the moment.

Why This Cookbook is Your Perfect New Year Companion

The Festive Flavors of New Year is more than a collection of recipes; it's a celebration of togetherness, creativity, and the joy of cooking. Whether you're hosting a grand New Year's Eve party, enjoying an intimate dinner with loved ones, or looking for comforting dishes to enjoy solo, this cookbook has something for everyone. The chapters are thoughtfully crafted to cater to diverse preferences and dietary needs, ensuring that every reader can find inspiration.

A Call to Embrace the New Year with Gratitude

As you embark on this culinary journey, let it be a reminder of the abundance and gratitude in your life. Each dish you prepare is an act of love and celebration, a way to connect with those around you and create memories that will linger long after the plates are cleared. The recipes in this book are a reflection of the resilience and joy we carry into each New Year, no matter what challenges the past year may have brought.

So, grab your apron, preheat the oven, and let's begin this journey together. The New Year is waiting to be welcomed, one delicious dish at a time. Cheers to a year filled with flavor, festivity, and culinary adventure!

Chapter 1: The Countdown Feast: Appetizers to Start the Year Right

As the anticipation of the New Year builds and the countdown begins, the perfect way to set the tone for the evening is with a spread of delectable appetizers. These small bites are more than just a prelude to the main course; they're an opportunity to excite the palate, spark conversation, and bring people together. In this chapter, you'll find recipes designed to impress, inspire, and delight your guests, ensuring the New Year's Eve celebration starts on a high note.

The Role of Appetizers in New Year's Celebrations

Appetizers serve a dual purpose at any gathering: they stave off hunger while setting the stage for the flavors to come. For New Year's Eve, they take on an even greater significance. This is the time when people are mingling, sipping on cocktails, and sharing their reflections on the year past. A well-thought-out selection of appetizers ensures there's something for everyone, creating an inclusive and inviting atmosphere.

From elegant canapés to hearty finger foods, appetizers for the New Year should reflect the festive spirit of the evening. They can be a nod to global traditions, incorporate symbolic ingredients for luck and prosperity, or simply showcase your creativity in the kitchen.

Essential Tips for an Appetizer Spread That Shines

1. **Variety is Key**: Offer a mix of textures, flavors, and temperatures. Combine creamy dips with crunchy chips, savory bites with a hint of sweetness, and warm dishes with cool offerings.
2. **Portion Control**: Appetizers should be easy to eat in one or two bites. This allows guests to mingle freely without needing utensils or plates.
3. **Prepare Ahead**: Many appetizers can be prepped in advance, allowing you to enjoy the evening with your guests rather than spending all your time in the kitchen.
4. **Visual Appeal**: Presentation matters. Use garnishes like fresh herbs, edible flowers, or colorful spices to make your appetizers look as enticing as they taste.

Recipes to Start the Year Right

1. Champagne-Infused Deviled Eggs

A sophisticated twist on a classic appetizer, these deviled eggs are elevated with the delicate flavor of champagne.

- **Ingredients**: Hard-boiled eggs, mayonnaise, Dijon mustard, champagne, chives, smoked paprika.
- **Directions**: Mix the egg yolks with mayonnaise, mustard, and a splash of champagne until smooth. Pipe the mixture back into the egg whites and garnish with chives and paprika.

2. Golden Cheese and Herb Pastry Twists

Symbolic of wealth and good fortune, these golden twists are a crowd-pleaser.

- **Ingredients**: Puff pastry, shredded Parmesan, fresh thyme, garlic powder, egg wash.
- **Directions**: Roll out puff pastry, sprinkle with cheese, thyme, and garlic powder. Fold, cut into strips, twist, and bake until golden.

3. Miniature Crab Cakes with Lemon Aioli

Perfectly crispy and bursting with flavor, these mini crab cakes are a luxurious start to the evening.

- **Ingredients**: Crab meat, breadcrumbs, egg, mayonnaise, Old Bay seasoning, lemon zest.
- **Directions**: Form small patties, fry until golden, and serve with a zesty lemon aioli.

4. Sparkling Fruit Skewers

A light and refreshing option, these skewers pair beautifully with champagne.

- **Ingredients**: Strawberries, grapes, pineapple chunks, edible gold dust.
- **Directions**: Thread fruit onto skewers, lightly brush with champagne, and sprinkle with gold dust.

5. Spiced Lentil Fritters

A nod to the Italian tradition of eating lentils for prosperity, these fritters are crispy on the outside and tender inside.

- **Ingredients**: Cooked lentils, onion, garlic, cumin, coriander, flour, egg.
- **Directions**: Combine all ingredients, form small fritters, and fry until golden. Serve with a tangy yogurt dip.

6. Asian-Inspired Lettuce Cups

Crisp lettuce leaves filled with savory and slightly sweet ground chicken make for a refreshing bite.

- **Ingredients**: Ground chicken, soy sauce, hoisin sauce, garlic, ginger, sesame oil, butter lettuce.
- **Directions**: Sauté chicken with seasonings, spoon into lettuce leaves, and top with chopped peanuts.

Pairing Appetizers with Drinks

The right beverage can elevate an appetizer to new heights. Here are a few pairing suggestions:

- **Champagne or Prosecco**: Perfect for light and creamy bites like deviled eggs or cheese twists.
- **Cocktails**: A citrusy cocktail complements seafood-based appetizers like crab cakes.
- **Mocktails**: For non-alcoholic options, pair fruit skewers with a sparkling water-based drink infused with mint and lime.

Creating a Countdown Moment

To make your appetizer spread even more special, consider timing certain dishes to be unveiled as the countdown approaches. Arrange your appetizers in a way that guides guests through a culinary journey, starting with lighter bites and building to more indulgent flavors.

The countdown to midnight is the most exciting part of the evening, and with these appetizers, you'll set the stage for a celebration to remember. Let this chapter inspire you to mix tradition with innovation, creating dishes that reflect the joy and hope of the New Year. Whether you're hosting an intimate gathering or a grand soirée, these recipes will ensure your guests start the evening—and the year—on a delicious note.

Chapter 2: Global New Year Traditions on a Plate

New Year's celebrations are as diverse as the cultures and traditions that shape them. Around the world, people ring in the New Year with foods that symbolize prosperity, longevity, love, and luck. Each dish carries a unique cultural significance, offering a glimpse into the values and hopes of different societies. In this chapter, we'll explore these global traditions and bring their vibrant flavors to your table, creating a feast that celebrates unity and the joy of shared traditions.

The Meaning of Food in New Year's Traditions

Food has always been central to New Year's rituals. Many cultures believe that what you eat at the start of the year can set the tone for the months ahead. From lentils in Italy to sticky rice cakes in Korea, the ingredients, preparation, and even the shapes of foods carry symbolic meanings.

Here are a few common themes found in New Year's foods:

- **Prosperity**: Golden or coin-shaped foods, like lentils or cornbread, symbolize wealth.
- **Longevity**: Long noodles or uncut foods represent long life.
- **Good Luck**: Round fruits and foods bring good fortune and unity.
- **Health and Abundance**: Leafy greens and hearty grains symbolize growth and well-being.

Recipes Inspired by Global Traditions

In this section, we'll recreate traditional New Year's dishes from around the world, with options for every skill level and taste.

1. Hoppin' John (Southern United States)

A classic dish of black-eyed peas and rice, often served with collard greens and cornbread, Hoppin' John is a Southern staple for New Year's Day, believed to bring wealth and luck.

- **Ingredients**: Black-eyed peas, smoked ham hock, long-grain rice, onions, garlic, chicken broth, collard greens.
- **Directions**: Simmer black-eyed peas with ham hock, onions, and garlic. Stir in rice and cook until tender. Serve with collard greens and cornbread for a complete meal.

2. Lentil Stew with Sausage (Italy)

In Italy, lentils are a symbol of prosperity because of their coin-like shape. Paired with sausage, this dish is hearty and satisfying.

- **Ingredients**: Lentils, Italian sausage, tomatoes, onions, garlic, olive oil, fresh parsley.
- **Directions**: Sauté sausage, onions, and garlic in olive oil. Add lentils and tomatoes, simmering until lentils are tender. Garnish with parsley.

3. 12 Grapes of Good Luck (Spain)

At the stroke of midnight, Spaniards eat 12 grapes, one for each chime of the clock, to ensure good luck for each month of the coming year.

- **Ingredients**: Green or red seedless grapes.
- **Directions**: Serve the grapes in small bunches or skewer them for easy eating during the countdown.

4. Soba Noodles (Japan)

Toshikoshi soba, or "year-crossing noodles," is a Japanese tradition that symbolizes letting go of the past and welcoming longevity in the New Year.

- **Ingredients**: Buckwheat soba noodles, soy sauce, mirin, dashi, green onions, seaweed.
- **Directions**: Cook soba noodles, then serve in a light soy-based broth topped with green onions and seaweed.

5. Sticky Rice Cake (Tteokguk) (Korea)

Eating Tteokguk, a soup with sliced rice cakes, is a Korean tradition that symbolizes a fresh start and the gaining of a year in age.

- **Ingredients**: Rice cakes, beef broth, garlic, soy sauce, eggs, green onions.
- **Directions**: Simmer rice cakes in beef broth with garlic and soy sauce. Garnish with a thinly sliced egg omelet and green onions.

6. Pomegranate Salad (Greece)

Pomegranates are a Greek symbol of fertility, abundance, and good luck. This vibrant salad incorporates the fruit's bright seeds.

- **Ingredients**: Pomegranate seeds, arugula, walnuts, feta cheese, balsamic vinaigrette.
- **Directions**: Toss all ingredients together and drizzle with vinaigrette for a fresh, tangy salad.

7. Whole Fish (China)

Serving a whole fish symbolizes abundance and surplus in the coming year. In Chinese tradition, it's important to leave some fish uneaten to carry over prosperity.

- **Ingredients**: Whole fish (such as sea bass), soy sauce, ginger, green onions, sesame oil.
- **Directions**: Steam or bake the fish with soy sauce, ginger, and sesame oil. Garnish with green onions before serving.

A Global Table

Creating a New Year's meal inspired by global traditions is not just about the food—it's about the stories, histories, and connections behind each dish. Here's how you can bring it all together:

1. **Plan a Themed Menu**: Select a variety of dishes from different countries to represent a global feast.
2. **Incorporate Symbolism**: Share the meanings behind each dish with your guests to create a deeper connection to the meal.
3. **Mix and Match**: Don't hesitate to combine flavors from different cultures—fusion cuisine is a celebration of unity.

Tips for Success

1. **Ingredient Substitutions**: If specific ingredients are hard to find, look for local alternatives that maintain the spirit of the dish.
2. **Presentation Matters**: Use decorative serving dishes and garnishes to reflect the culture of each recipe.
3. **Celebrate Inclusivity**: Provide options for various dietary needs so everyone can enjoy the feast.

The Spirit of Unity

As you prepare your global New Year's feast, remember that food is a bridge that connects us all. By incorporating traditions from around the world, you're not only honoring diverse cultures but also embracing the shared hope and joy that unites us in welcoming a new year. Let your table be a reflection of this beautiful tapestry of flavors, stories, and traditions.

Chapter 3: Champagne Pairings and Sparkling Cocktails

No New Year's celebration is complete without the effervescent pop of a champagne cork. Champagne and sparkling beverages are synonymous with joy, luxury, and celebration, making them the perfect centerpiece for your festivities. In this chapter, we'll dive into the art of pairing champagne with food, creating dazzling cocktails, and understanding how to choose the right sparkling wine for any occasion. Whether you're hosting a grand party or enjoying an intimate gathering, this guide will elevate your New Year's experience.

Why Champagne?

Champagne is more than just a drink; it's a symbol of celebration and new beginnings. The crisp, bubbly nature of champagne enhances flavors, cleanses the palate, and brings an air of sophistication to any event. While traditional champagne comes from the Champagne region of France, sparkling wines like Prosecco, Cava, and other brut options can also deliver that signature sparkle without breaking the bank.

Understanding Champagne Styles

Before diving into pairings and cocktails, let's explore the different types of champagne and sparkling wine:

1. **Brut**: Dry and crisp, ideal for savory dishes and light appetizers.
2. **Extra Brut**: Even drier than Brut, great for rich, creamy foods.
3. **Demi-Sec**: Slightly sweet, perfect for desserts and fruit-based dishes.
4. **Rosé Champagne**: Offers notes of berries and floral undertones, pairing beautifully with both savory and sweet options.

Champagne Pairings

Pairing champagne with food is all about balance. The goal is to complement the flavors of the dish without overpowering them.

1. Light Appetizers

- **Pair with**: Brut Champagne
- **Examples**: Smoked salmon canapés, oysters on the half shell, or goat cheese crostini.
- **Why It Works**: The acidity of Brut cuts through the richness of smoked and creamy foods, while the bubbles cleanse the palate.

2. Savory Mains

- **Pair with**: Rosé Champagne
- **Examples**: Herb-crusted chicken, grilled salmon, or mushroom risotto.
- **Why It Works**: Rosé's fruity undertones balance the earthy and umami flavors of these dishes.

3. Fried Foods

- **Pair with**: Extra Brut Champagne
- **Examples**: Tempura vegetables, fried chicken, or potato croquettes.
- **Why It Works**: The high acidity of Extra Brut complements the greasiness of fried foods, offering a refreshing contrast.

4. Desserts

- **Pair with**: Demi-Sec Champagne
- **Examples**: Fruit tarts, macarons, or white chocolate mousse.
- **Why It Works**: The slight sweetness of Demi-Sec harmonizes with sugary desserts, enhancing their flavors.

5. Cheese Platters

- **Pair with**: Brut or Rosé Champagne
- **Examples**: Brie, Gruyère, or aged Parmesan.
- **Why It Works**: The effervescence of champagne balances the richness of cheese while highlighting its nutty or tangy notes.

Sparkling Cocktails

Sparkling cocktails bring creativity and flair to your New Year's menu. These recipes are quick, easy, and guaranteed to impress your guests.

1. Classic Mimosa

A brunch favorite that's perfect for a light and fruity toast.

- **Ingredients**: Equal parts Brut Champagne and orange juice.
- **Directions**: Pour the orange juice into a flute and top with champagne. Garnish with a slice of orange.

2. Kir Royale

A sophisticated French cocktail with a touch of sweetness.

- **Ingredients**: 1 teaspoon crème de cassis, Brut Champagne.
- **Directions**: Add crème de cassis to a flute and top with champagne. Garnish with a fresh berry.

3. Pomegranate Sparkle

Festive and colorful, this cocktail is ideal for New Year's Eve.

- **Ingredients**: Brut Champagne, pomegranate juice, pomegranate seeds.
- **Directions**: Add a splash of pomegranate juice to a flute, top with champagne, and sprinkle in a few pomegranate seeds.

4. French 75

A classic cocktail with a citrusy kick.

- **Ingredients**: 1 ounce gin, ½ ounce lemon juice, ½ ounce simple syrup, Brut Champagne.
- **Directions**: Shake gin, lemon juice, and simple syrup with ice, strain into a flute, and top with champagne. Garnish with a lemon twist.

5. Sparkling Mojito

A bubbly twist on the refreshing mojito.

- **Ingredients**: Fresh mint, 1 teaspoon sugar, ½ ounce lime juice, Prosecco or Brut Champagne.
- **Directions**: Muddle mint, sugar, and lime juice in a glass. Top with champagne and garnish with a mint sprig.

Creating the Perfect Champagne Bar

For an interactive and engaging New Year's Eve setup, consider creating a champagne bar where guests can mix their own sparkling cocktails. Here's what you'll need:

1. **Champagne Selection**: Offer a mix of Brut, Rosé, and Demi-Sec.
2. **Juices and Mixers**: Orange juice, cranberry juice, pomegranate juice, and simple syrups.
3. **Fresh Garnishes**: Citrus slices, berries, mint, and edible flowers.
4. **Glassware**: Champagne flutes and coupes for a touch of elegance.

Tips for Serving Champagne

1. **Temperature Matters**: Serve champagne chilled at 45-48°F (7-9°C) for optimal flavor and bubbles.
2. **Opening with Style**: Hold the cork firmly and twist the bottle, not the cork, to avoid spills.
3. **The Right Glass**: Use flutes to concentrate the bubbles and aroma, or coupes for a retro aesthetic.

Ending the Evening on a Sparkling Note

Whether you're toasting to the New Year with a classic champagne flute or sipping on a vibrant cocktail, sparkling beverages add a sense of magic to the celebration. The versatility of champagne allows it to shine on its own, pair beautifully with food, or transform into a dazzling cocktail. Let this chapter inspire you to experiment and create a menu that sparkles as brightly as the fireworks in the sky. Cheers to a year of flavor, joy, and unforgettable memories!

Chapter 4: Lucky Foods for Prosperity and Health

Across the globe, people have long believed in the power of food to bring luck, health, and prosperity in the New Year. These traditions, rooted in culture and symbolism, guide the dishes served during the celebration. In this chapter, we explore the fascinating stories behind these foods and provide detailed recipes to incorporate them into your New Year's feast. Whether you're seeking financial fortune, good health, or general well-being, these dishes are steeped in meaning and brimming with flavor.

The Symbolism of Lucky Foods

The belief in "lucky" foods stems from the idea that certain ingredients, shapes, colors, or preparation methods can attract positive energy. Here are some common themes associated with lucky foods:

- **Wealth**: Golden-colored or coin-shaped foods symbolize money and prosperity.
- **Health**: Leafy greens and hearty grains represent growth and vitality.
- **Long Life**: Long noodles or unbroken foods symbolize longevity.
- **Unity and Harmony**: Round or circular foods signify completeness and unity.

Lucky Foods from Around the World

Here's a guide to traditional lucky foods and how to incorporate them into your New Year's menu.

1. Black-Eyed Peas (Southern United States)

A staple in Southern New Year's celebrations, black-eyed peas are said to bring prosperity and luck. They are often paired with collard greens to symbolize wealth.

- **Dish Idea**: Black-Eyed Pea Salad with Lemon Vinaigrette
  - **Ingredients**: Black-eyed peas, cherry tomatoes, red onion, parsley, olive oil, lemon juice, Dijon mustard.
  - **Directions**: Toss cooked black-eyed peas with diced tomatoes, onions, and parsley. Whisk olive oil, lemon juice, and mustard for the vinaigrette, then mix into the salad.

2. Lentils (Italy)

In Italy, lentils are associated with wealth because their shape resembles coins. They are often served with sausages, symbolizing abundance.

- **Dish Idea**: Lentil and Sausage Stew
  - **Ingredients**: Lentils, Italian sausage, tomatoes, carrots, celery, garlic, chicken broth, olive oil.
  - **Directions**: Sauté sausages and vegetables in olive oil. Add lentils and broth, simmering until the lentils are tender.

3. Greens (Global)

Leafy greens, such as collard greens, kale, or cabbage, symbolize money due to their green color and folded shape, which resembles cash.

- **Dish Idea**: Garlic Sautéed Collard Greens
    - **Ingredients**: Collard greens, garlic, olive oil, red pepper flakes, lemon juice.
    - **Directions**: Sauté minced garlic in olive oil, add chopped collard greens, and cook until tender. Finish with a squeeze of lemon juice.

4. Noodles (Asia)

In many Asian cultures, long noodles represent long life. The key is to cook and serve them uncut to preserve their symbolic meaning.

- **Dish Idea**: Stir-Fried Longevity Noodles
    - **Ingredients**: Long wheat noodles, soy sauce, sesame oil, ginger, garlic, green onions, vegetables (e.g., carrots, bell peppers), chicken or shrimp.
    - **Directions**: Stir-fry ginger, garlic, and vegetables in sesame oil. Add cooked noodles and protein, then toss with soy sauce.

5. Fish (China and Europe)

A whole fish symbolizes abundance and surplus in the New Year, especially when the head and tail are left intact, representing a good beginning and end to the year.

- **Dish Idea**: Steamed Whole Fish with Ginger and Scallions
    - **Ingredients**: Whole sea bass, soy sauce, ginger, garlic, sesame oil, scallions, cilantro.
    - **Directions**: Steam the fish with ginger and garlic, then drizzle with soy sauce and sesame oil. Garnish with scallions and cilantro.

6. Pomegranates (Mediterranean)

In countries like Greece and Turkey, pomegranates symbolize fertility, abundance, and good luck due to their many seeds.

- **Dish Idea**: Pomegranate and Walnut Salad
    - **Ingredients**: Pomegranate seeds, mixed greens, walnuts, feta cheese, balsamic vinaigrette.
    - **Directions**: Toss greens with pomegranate seeds, walnuts, and feta. Drizzle with balsamic vinaigrette.

7. Round Cakes and Breads (Global)

Circular cakes or breads, such as King's Cake or cornbread, represent the cycle of life and unity. Some cultures even bake a coin or trinket inside for added luck.

- **Dish Idea**: Honey Cornbread
    - **Ingredients**: Cornmeal, flour, honey, butter, eggs, baking powder, milk.
    - **Directions**: Mix dry ingredients, then add wet ingredients and bake until golden. Optionally, bake a small trinket inside (ensure it's safe for food).

8. Grapes (Spain and Latin America)

Eating 12 grapes at midnight—one for each chime of the clock—ensures good luck for all 12 months of the year.

- **Dish Idea**: Grapes in Champagne Jelly
    - **Ingredients**: Seedless grapes, champagne, sugar, gelatin.
    - **Directions**: Dissolve gelatin in champagne and sugar, pour over grapes in a mold, and refrigerate until set.

9. Rice (Global)

Rice is a universal symbol of abundance, fertility, and sustenance.

- **Dish Idea**: Coconut Rice with Toasted Almonds
    - **Ingredients**: Jasmine rice, coconut milk, water, toasted almonds, salt.
    - **Directions**: Cook rice in coconut milk and water, then top with toasted almonds for added texture.

Crafting a Lucky New Year's Menu

To create a cohesive menu featuring lucky foods, consider these combinations:

1. **Appetizer**: Pomegranate and Walnut Salad with a Champagne Vinaigrette.
2. **Main Course**: Steamed Whole Fish served with Stir-Fried Longevity Noodles and Garlic Sautéed Collard Greens.
3. **Dessert**: Honey Cornbread with a hidden trinket or Grapes in Champagne Jelly.

Tips for Incorporating Lucky Foods

1. **Highlight Symbolism**: Share the meaning behind each dish with your guests to create a meaningful dining experience.
2. **Balance Flavors**: Ensure your menu has a mix of savory, sweet, and tangy elements.
3. **Presentation Matters**: Use garnishes like edible flowers, herbs, or colorful fruits to enhance the visual appeal.
4. **Involve Guests**: Encourage guests to try foods from different cultures to embrace the spirit of unity and diversity.

The Spirit of Prosperity and Health

As you enjoy these lucky dishes, remember that their power lies not just in tradition but also in the intention and love with which they are prepared. By incorporating these foods into your New Year's celebration, you're not only honoring age-old customs but also setting a hopeful tone for the year ahead. May your table be abundant, your health robust, and your fortune plentiful. Cheers to prosperity, health, and the joy of sharing delicious food!

Chapter 5: Midnight Bites: Snacks to Welcome the New Year

As the countdown reaches its final seconds and the New Year begins, the focus shifts to celebration and indulgence. Midnight snacks serve as the perfect way to keep the energy alive, providing festive bites that satisfy cravings, pair well with drinks, and encourage laughter and conversation. These snacks are more than just food—they're a part of the memories being made, shared as the clock strikes twelve and beyond.

In this chapter, you'll find a curated selection of savory, sweet, and creative midnight bites designed to elevate your New Year's festivities. These recipes are easy to prepare, visually stunning, and full of flavor, ensuring your celebration is as vibrant as the fireworks lighting up the sky.

The Role of Midnight Snacks

Midnight snacks are integral to keeping the momentum of a New Year's party. They:

1. **Keep Guests Energized**: Small, flavorful bites help refuel partygoers as they dance and celebrate into the early hours.
2. **Complement Drinks**: These snacks are designed to pair with the champagne, cocktails, and mocktails served throughout the evening.
3. **Add to the Festive Atmosphere**: Fun, creative presentations make midnight snacks part of the entertainment.

Tips for Perfect Midnight Snacks

1. **Portion Control**: Snacks should be bite-sized and easy to eat without utensils. Think finger foods and skewers.
2. **Make Ahead**: Prepare as much as possible beforehand to minimize time spent in the kitchen during the party.
3. **Balanced Menu**: Include a mix of flavors—salty, sweet, tangy, and spicy—to cater to all tastes.
4. **Presentation Matters**: Use decorative serving trays, edible garnishes, and creative plating to make the snacks visually appealing.

Savory Midnight Bites

1. Mini Caprese Skewers

A refreshing, no-cook option that's as visually appealing as it is delicious.

- **Ingredients**: Cherry tomatoes, fresh mozzarella balls, basil leaves, balsamic glaze, skewers.
- **Directions**: Thread a cherry tomato, basil leaf, and mozzarella ball onto each skewer. Drizzle with balsamic glaze before serving.

2. Crispy Parmesan Truffle Fries

A luxurious take on a party classic.

- **Ingredients**: Russet potatoes, truffle oil, grated Parmesan, parsley, salt.
- **Directions**: Slice potatoes into thin fries, bake until crispy, then toss with truffle oil, Parmesan, and parsley.

3. Spicy Chicken Meatballs

Juicy and flavorful, these meatballs pack a punch of spice.

- **Ingredients**: Ground chicken, breadcrumbs, egg, garlic, chili flakes, sriracha, soy sauce.
- **Directions**: Mix all ingredients, form into bite-sized meatballs, and bake until golden. Serve with a spicy dipping sauce.

4. Loaded Nacho Cups

A single-serve twist on classic nachos.

- **Ingredients**: Tortilla chips, shredded cheese, black beans, diced tomatoes, jalapeños, sour cream, guacamole.
- **Directions**: Arrange chips in muffin tins, layer with toppings, and bake until the cheese is melted. Top with sour cream and guacamole.

5. Savory Puff Pastry Pinwheels

Flaky, buttery pastry filled with delicious savory ingredients.

- **Ingredients**: Puff pastry, sun-dried tomatoes, spinach, feta cheese, garlic.
- **Directions**: Spread filling on rolled-out pastry, roll tightly, slice into pinwheels, and bake until golden.

Sweet Midnight Treats
1. Chocolate-Dipped Strawberries
Elegant and easy, these are a perennial favorite.

- **Ingredients**: Fresh strawberries, dark chocolate, white chocolate (optional for drizzle).
- **Directions**: Dip strawberries in melted chocolate, allow to set, and drizzle with white chocolate for decoration.

2. Mini Cheesecake Bites
Rich, creamy, and perfectly portioned.

- **Ingredients**: Graham cracker crumbs, cream cheese, sugar, vanilla, eggs, fresh berries.
- **Directions**: Press crumbs into a mini muffin tin, fill with cheesecake mixture, and bake. Top with berries or jam.

3. Midnight Macarons
Delicate cookies filled with buttercream or ganache.

- **Ingredients**: Almond flour, powdered sugar, egg whites, sugar, food coloring, buttercream or ganache filling.
- **Directions**: Whisk egg whites with sugar to form a meringue, fold in almond flour mixture, pipe onto a baking sheet, and bake. Fill with desired filling.

4. Sparkling Sugar Cookies
Glittering cookies perfect for the occasion.

- **Ingredients**: Sugar cookie dough, royal icing, edible glitter.
- **Directions**: Bake cookies, decorate with icing, and sprinkle with edible glitter for a festive touch.

5. Champagne Jello Shots
A fun, grown-up twist on a party favorite.

- **Ingredients**: Champagne, gelatin, sugar, edible gold stars (optional).
- **Directions**: Dissolve gelatin in champagne and sugar, pour into molds, and refrigerate. Decorate with edible gold stars.

Creative and Thematic Snacks
1. Midnight Sliders
Miniature burgers that pack big flavor.

- **Ingredients**: Ground beef, slider buns, cheddar cheese, pickles, ketchup, mustard.
- **Directions**: Grill patties, assemble sliders with toppings, and serve with a side of fries.

2. Firecracker Shrimp Skewers
Spicy shrimp with a kick to energize your guests.

- **Ingredients**: Shrimp, chili powder, lime juice, garlic, skewers.
- **Directions**: Marinate shrimp, thread onto skewers, and grill or sauté until cooked.

3. Popcorn Trio
Offer a variety of flavors to please every palate.

- **Flavors**: Truffle Parmesan, caramel, spicy chili lime.
- **Directions**: Prepare popcorn, toss each batch with its respective flavorings, and serve in decorative bowls.

Pairing Snacks with Midnight Drinks
The right drink enhances the midnight snack experience:

- **Champagne Pairings**: Mini Caprese Skewers, Chocolate-Dipped Strawberries.
- **Cocktail Pairings**: Spicy Chicken Meatballs with a spicy margarita or loaded nacho cups with a mojito.
- **Mocktail Pairings**: Sparkling Sugar Cookies with a berry-infused sparkling water.

Creating a Midnight Snack Station
For a hassle-free approach, set up a self-serve snack station:

1. **Label Foods**: Use small cards to label each snack.
2. **Provide Utensils**: Offer skewers, toothpicks, or small plates for easy serving.
3. **Decorate**: Incorporate New Year's-themed decorations like glittering tablecloths, candles, or confetti.

Midnight Snacks for a Memorable New Year

As the New Year unfolds, these midnight bites ensure your guests remain energized and delighted. Each snack is designed to celebrate the occasion, keeping the festive atmosphere alive well past the stroke of midnight. With this chapter as your guide, you'll create a spread that sparks joy, satisfies cravings, and leaves a lasting impression as you welcome the New Year. Cheers to midnight memories and delicious bites!

Chapter 6: Hearty Soups for the New Year Chill

As the festivities of the New Year unfold, the chill of winter often lingers in the air, making hearty soups the perfect addition to your celebration. Warm, comforting, and nourishing, soups offer a way to bring people together and provide much-needed sustenance after a night of revelry. This chapter explores a variety of hearty soups from around the world, perfect for welcoming the New Year with a steaming bowl of goodness.

From creamy bisques to chunky stews, these recipes are designed to satisfy cravings, warm the soul, and symbolize prosperity, health, and comfort. Whether served as a light starter or a main dish, these soups will be a hit with your guests.

Why Soups are Perfect for the New Year

1. **Warmth and Comfort**: Soups are ideal for combating the winter chill and providing a sense of coziness.
2. **Versatility**: They can be customized to fit dietary preferences, using whatever ingredients you have on hand.
3. **Symbolism**: Many traditional soups feature ingredients that symbolize luck, prosperity, and health in various cultures.

Tips for Making Perfect Soups

1. **Build Depth of Flavor**: Use a base of sautéed onions, garlic, and celery, then add layers of seasoning, herbs, and spices.
2. **Choose Quality Stock**: A good broth or stock forms the foundation of any great soup. Homemade is best, but high-quality store-bought options work well.
3. **Add Textural Variety**: Combine soft and crunchy elements, such as croutons, toasted seeds, or fresh herbs, for a satisfying eating experience.
4. **Serve Fresh**: Soups often taste better after resting, so prepare them ahead and reheat for optimal flavor.

Hearty Soup Recipes for the New Year

1. Classic Black-Eyed Pea Soup (Southern United States)

Symbolizing luck and prosperity, this hearty soup is a staple in Southern New Year's celebrations.

- **Ingredients**: Black-eyed peas, smoked ham hock, onions, celery, garlic, carrots, chicken broth, collard greens.
- **Directions**: Sauté vegetables, then simmer black-eyed peas and ham hock in chicken broth until tender. Add collard greens near the end of cooking.

2. Italian Lentil Soup (Italy)

Lentils, resembling coins, are eaten in Italy to bring wealth in the New Year.

- **Ingredients**: Lentils, Italian sausage, tomatoes, onions, garlic, carrots, celery, olive oil, fresh parsley.
- **Directions**: Brown sausage in olive oil, then add vegetables and lentils. Simmer with tomatoes and broth until lentils are tender. Garnish with parsley.

3. Japanese Miso Soup with Long Noodles (Japan)

This soup features unbroken noodles, symbolizing long life and good fortune.

- **Ingredients**: Miso paste, dashi stock, tofu, wakame seaweed, scallions, soba noodles.
- **Directions**: Dissolve miso paste in warm dashi stock. Add tofu and wakame, then serve over cooked soba noodles. Garnish with scallions.

4. French Onion Soup (France)

Rich and indulgent, this classic soup is perfect for a New Year's treat.

- **Ingredients**: Yellow onions, beef broth, dry white wine, butter, thyme, baguette slices, Gruyère cheese.
- **Directions**: Caramelize onions in butter, deglaze with wine, then simmer with beef broth and thyme. Serve with toasted baguette slices topped with melted Gruyère.

5. Spicy Tom Yum Soup (Thailand)

This tangy and spicy soup is perfect for warming up a crowd.

- **Ingredients**: Lemongrass, lime leaves, galangal, shrimp, mushrooms, fish sauce, chili paste, lime juice, cilantro.
- **Directions**: Simmer lemongrass, lime leaves, and galangal in broth. Add shrimp and mushrooms, then finish with fish sauce, chili paste, and lime juice.

6. Creamy Butternut Squash Soup (Global)

Sweet and velvety, this soup is both comforting and elegant.

- **Ingredients**: Butternut squash, onions, garlic, vegetable broth, cream, nutmeg, olive oil.
- **Directions**: Roast squash with olive oil until caramelized. Blend with sautéed onions, garlic, and broth. Stir in cream and season with nutmeg.

7. Borscht (Eastern Europe)

A vibrant beet soup that symbolizes vitality and strength.

- **Ingredients**: Beets, potatoes, carrots, onions, cabbage, dill, sour cream.
- **Directions**: Simmer beets and vegetables in broth until tender. Serve with a dollop of sour cream and a sprinkle of fresh dill.

8. Creamy Clam Chowder (New England)

Rich and hearty, this soup is perfect for coastal New Year's celebrations.

- **Ingredients**: Clams, potatoes, celery, onions, bacon, heavy cream, butter, thyme.
- **Directions**: Sauté bacon and vegetables in butter, add clams and potatoes, then stir in cream and seasonings.

9. Mulligatawny Soup (India)

This spiced lentil and rice soup is warming and flavorful.

- **Ingredients**: Red lentils, basmati rice, chicken, curry powder, coconut milk, onions, garlic, ginger.
- **Directions**: Sauté spices with onions, garlic, and ginger. Add lentils, rice, chicken, and broth. Simmer, then stir in coconut milk.

10. Hungarian Goulash Soup (Hungary)

A robust and flavorful stew-like soup that symbolizes strength and resilience.

- **Ingredients**: Beef, onions, garlic, paprika, potatoes, carrots, tomatoes, caraway seeds.
- **Directions**: Brown beef with onions and garlic, add spices and vegetables, and simmer until tender.

Enhancements for Hearty Soups

1. **Bread Pairings**: Serve with crusty bread, garlic knots, or breadsticks for a complete meal.
2. **Garnishes**: Fresh herbs, grated cheese, or a swirl of cream add an elegant touch.
3. **Sides**: Pair with simple salads or roasted vegetables for a well-rounded meal.

Creating a Soup Station

For a New Year's gathering, consider setting up a soup station:

1. **Serve Multiple Options**: Offer 2–3 soup varieties to cater to different preferences.
2. **Self-Serve Setup**: Provide ladles, bowls, and toppings for guests to customize their soup.
3. **Themed Décor**: Use winter-themed accents like snowflake napkins or rustic serving pots to enhance the presentation.

The Heartwarming Power of Soup

Hearty soups not only warm the body but also nourish the soul, making them an essential part of any New Year's celebration. These recipes bring together tradition, flavor, and symbolism, ensuring your table is filled with dishes that embody prosperity, health, and comfort. Let the aroma of these hearty soups fill your home, inviting warmth, togetherness, and joy as you welcome the New Year.

Chapter 7: Salad Creations for Fresh Beginnings

As the New Year dawns, it symbolizes a fresh start, making salads a perfect metaphor and addition to your celebration menu. Bright, crisp, and bursting with vibrant flavors, salads are more than just a side dish—they represent health, renewal, and vitality. In this chapter, we'll explore creative salad recipes that are as delightful to eat as they are beautiful to behold. These dishes highlight fresh ingredients, global flavors, and symbolic touches, setting the tone for a prosperous year ahead.

Why Salads for the New Year?

1. **Symbolism**: Fresh greens, colorful vegetables, and hearty grains embody abundance, health, and growth.
2. **Versatility**: Salads can be customized for any dietary preference, ensuring inclusivity at your table.
3. **Light and Refreshing**: After the indulgent holiday season, salads offer a refreshing and healthy balance.

Salad Essentials for Success

1. **Texture**: Balance crunchy, creamy, and soft ingredients for an enjoyable eating experience.
2. **Flavors**: Combine sweet, salty, tangy, and bitter elements to create depth.
3. **Visual Appeal**: Use a variety of colors and shapes to make the salad visually enticing.
4. **Dressings**: The right dressing can elevate a salad. Balance oil, acid, and seasonings for a harmonious flavor.

Salad Recipes for Fresh Beginnings

1. Classic New Year's Pomegranate Salad

Symbolizing prosperity and abundance, pomegranate seeds add a festive and flavorful touch to this salad.

- **Ingredients**: Mixed greens (arugula, spinach, and kale), pomegranate seeds, walnuts, feta cheese, balsamic vinaigrette.
- **Directions**: Toss greens with pomegranate seeds, toasted walnuts, and crumbled feta. Drizzle with balsamic vinaigrette before serving.

2. Citrus and Avocado Salad

Bright and zesty, this salad represents energy and freshness for the year ahead.

- **Ingredients**: Orange and grapefruit segments, sliced avocado, red onion, mixed greens, olive oil, lime juice, honey.
- **Directions**: Arrange citrus segments, avocado slices, and onion over greens. Whisk olive oil, lime juice, and honey for the dressing, then drizzle over the salad.

3. Lentil and Quinoa Salad

Packed with protein and fiber, this hearty salad is a nod to health and prosperity.

- **Ingredients**: Cooked lentils, quinoa, diced cucumber, cherry tomatoes, parsley, olive oil, lemon juice, cumin.
- **Directions**: Combine lentils, quinoa, and vegetables. Toss with a dressing made from olive oil, lemon juice, and cumin. Garnish with parsley.

4. Asian-Inspired Noodle Salad

Long noodles symbolize longevity, making this salad a meaningful and delicious choice.

- **Ingredients**: Rice noodles, shredded carrots, julienned bell peppers, cilantro, sesame seeds, soy sauce, sesame oil, rice vinegar.
- **Directions**: Cook noodles and toss with vegetables. Mix soy sauce, sesame oil, and rice vinegar for the dressing. Garnish with sesame seeds.

5. Caprese Salad with a Twist

A refreshing Italian classic that symbolizes harmony and balance.

- **Ingredients**: Fresh mozzarella, cherry tomatoes, basil leaves, balsamic reduction, olive oil, mixed greens.
- **Directions**: Layer mozzarella, tomatoes, and basil on a bed of greens. Drizzle with olive oil and balsamic reduction.

6. Winter Harvest Salad

This salad celebrates seasonal produce, offering a rustic and hearty flavor profile.

- **Ingredients**: Roasted butternut squash, kale, dried cranberries, toasted pecans, goat cheese, apple cider vinaigrette.
- **Directions**: Massage kale with a bit of olive oil to soften. Add roasted squash, cranberries, pecans, and goat cheese. Drizzle with apple cider vinaigrette.

7. Mediterranean Chickpea Salad

A vibrant, protein-packed salad perfect for any New Year's spread.

- **Ingredients**: Chickpeas, diced cucumber, cherry tomatoes, red onion, olives, feta cheese, oregano, lemon vinaigrette.
- **Directions**: Toss chickpeas and vegetables with crumbled feta and oregano. Add lemon vinaigrette before serving.

8. Sweet and Savory Apple Salad

Crisp apples and sharp cheddar cheese create a delightful contrast in this flavorful salad.

- **Ingredients**: Sliced apples, sharp cheddar cubes, mixed greens, candied pecans, Dijon vinaigrette.
- **Directions**: Arrange apples, cheddar, and pecans over greens. Whisk Dijon mustard, olive oil, and apple cider vinegar for the dressing, and drizzle before serving.

9. Grilled Vegetable Salad

A smoky and hearty salad that's perfect for winter.

- **Ingredients**: Zucchini, bell peppers, eggplant, red onions, mixed greens, olive oil, balsamic glaze.
- **Directions**: Grill vegetables until tender, then slice and serve over greens. Drizzle with balsamic glaze.

10. Creamy Cucumber and Dill Salad

Refreshing and light, this salad is a palate cleanser and a crowd favorite.

- **Ingredients**: Sliced cucumbers, Greek yogurt, dill, garlic, lemon juice, salt, pepper.
- **Directions**: Toss cucumbers with yogurt, dill, garlic, and lemon juice. Season with salt and pepper.

Making Salads Shine: Toppings and Dressings
Topping Ideas:

- **Crunch**: Toasted nuts, seeds, or croutons.
- **Sweetness**: Dried fruits like cranberries, raisins, or figs.
- **Freshness**: Chopped herbs like basil, mint, or parsley.
- **Protein**: Grilled chicken, tofu, or boiled eggs.

Dressings:

1. **Classic Vinaigrette**: Whisk olive oil, vinegar, Dijon mustard, and honey.
2. **Creamy Ranch**: Combine Greek yogurt, buttermilk, garlic, and herbs.
3. **Tahini Dressing**: Blend tahini, lemon juice, garlic, and water until smooth.
4. **Citrus Glaze**: Mix orange juice, olive oil, and a touch of honey.

Creating a Salad Bar for Your New Year's Party

For an interactive and customizable option, set up a salad bar:

1. **Base Options**: Offer greens like spinach, kale, and romaine.
2. **Toppings**: Provide a variety of vegetables, fruits, nuts, and proteins.
3. **Dressings**: Include 3–4 dressing options to cater to different tastes.
4. **Presentation**: Arrange ingredients in clear bowls for an appealing setup.

Why Fresh Beginnings Matter

Salads are more than a dish—they're a statement of renewal, health, and intention. By incorporating these creations into your New Year's celebration, you're embracing the spirit of fresh starts and vibrant possibilities. Whether served as a starter, side, or main, these salads will leave your guests feeling nourished and inspired for the year ahead. Let your table bloom with the colors, textures, and flavors of these creations as you celebrate a new beginning.

Chapter 8: Bread for Breaking: Traditional New Year Loaves

Bread has long been a symbol of sustenance, unity, and prosperity, making it a cherished part of New Year's celebrations around the world. Whether it's a sweet loaf shared among family or a savory bread baked to bring good fortune, the tradition of breaking bread is both a culinary and cultural gesture of togetherness. In this chapter, we'll explore the stories, significance, and recipes behind traditional New Year loaves that you can bake and share to welcome the coming year with warmth and abundance.

The Significance of Bread in New Year Traditions

Bread has played a vital role in human history as a staple food and a symbol of life. For New Year's, bread often carries additional meanings:

1. **Prosperity and Abundance**: Ingredients like honey, spices, or seeds represent wealth and fertility.
2. **Unity and Sharing**: The act of breaking and sharing bread symbolizes community and connection.
3. **Luck and Fortune**: Hidden tokens or specific shapes are believed to bring blessings and good luck.

Traditional New Year Loaves Around the World

1. Vasilopita (Greece)

This sweet bread is baked with a coin hidden inside, symbolizing luck for the year ahead.

- **Ingredients**: All-purpose flour, sugar, milk, eggs, yeast, orange zest, butter.
- **Directions**:
  1. Prepare a sweet yeast dough and let it rise.
  2. Shape into a round loaf, hiding a wrapped coin in the dough.
  3. Bake until golden and dust with powdered sugar before serving.
  4. **Tradition**: The loaf is sliced, and the person who finds the coin is said to have good fortune.

2. Rosca de Reyes (Mexico)

This ring-shaped sweet bread is topped with candied fruit and traditionally eaten on Epiphany (January 6th).

- **Ingredients**: Bread flour, sugar, eggs, butter, orange zest, candied fruits.
- **Directions**:
  1. Make a rich, egg-based dough. Shape it into a ring and decorate with candied fruit.
  2. Bake until golden and drizzle with a light glaze.
  3. **Tradition**: A small figurine is baked into the bread. Whoever finds it hosts the next celebration.

3. Challah (Jewish Tradition)

This braided bread, often served on Shabbat and holidays, is made round for Rosh Hashanah to symbolize the cycle of the year.

- **Ingredients**: Bread flour, eggs, sugar, yeast, water, oil, sesame seeds.
- **Directions**:
    1. Prepare a slightly sweet dough, let it rise, and braid it.
    2. Shape into a round loaf and sprinkle with sesame seeds before baking.
    3. **Symbolism**: The round shape represents the endless cycle of time.

4. Irish Soda Bread (Ireland)

Quick and simple to make, soda bread symbolizes simplicity and sustenance.

- **Ingredients**: Flour, baking soda, buttermilk, salt, raisins (optional).
- **Directions**:
    1. Mix dry ingredients, then stir in buttermilk until a soft dough forms.
    2. Shape into a round loaf, score a cross on top, and bake.
    3. **Tradition**: The cross is said to ward off evil spirits.

5. Hoppin' John Cornbread (Southern United States)

Cornbread is often served alongside Hoppin' John for a New Year meal, symbolizing gold and wealth.

- **Ingredients**: Cornmeal, flour, eggs, buttermilk, butter, sugar (optional).
- **Directions**:
    1. Combine ingredients to make a thick batter.
    2. Pour into a hot, greased skillet and bake until golden.
    3. **Tip**: Add diced jalapeños or cheese for a savory twist.

6. Panettone (Italy)

This tall, dome-shaped sweet bread is filled with dried fruits and enjoyed during the holiday season.

- **Ingredients**: Bread flour, eggs, butter, sugar, dried fruits, yeast.
- **Directions**:
    1. Mix a rich dough and let it rise multiple times for an airy texture.
    2. Bake in a tall pan until golden and serve in slices.
    3. **Tradition**: Often gifted to symbolize abundance and goodwill.

7. Tsoureki (Greece)

Similar to challah but flavored with spices like mahleb or cardamom, this bread is often braided.

- **Ingredients**: Bread flour, sugar, eggs, butter, mahleb, yeast.
- **Directions**:
    1. Prepare a spiced dough, braid it, and let it rise.
    2. Bake until golden and brush with a syrup glaze.
    3. **Symbolism**: Its sweetness represents hope for a joyful year.

Techniques for Perfect New Year Loaves

1. **Use Fresh Ingredients**: Active yeast and fresh flour ensure a better rise and flavor.
2. **Proof Properly**: Allow the dough to rise in a warm, draft-free place for the best texture.
3. **Shape Creatively**: Experiment with braiding, rings, or round shapes to add festive flair.
4. **Decorate Thoughtfully**: Use seeds, nuts, or dried fruits for a visually appealing finish.

Modern Twists on Traditional Loaves

1. **Savory Herb Bread**: Incorporate rosemary, thyme, and garlic into a classic loaf.
2. **Chocolate Swirl Bread**: Add a layer of chocolate and cinnamon to sweet dough before rolling and baking.
3. **Vegan-Friendly Options**: Substitute dairy and eggs with plant-based alternatives for inclusivity.
4. **Gluten-Free Versions**: Use gluten-free flours like almond or rice flour for those with dietary restrictions.

Serving Suggestions and Pairings

1. **Breakfast Spread**: Serve sweet breads with butter, honey, or jam.
2. **Appetizer Platter**: Pair savory loaves with dips, cheeses, or cured meats.
3. **Main Meal Side**: Use breads like cornbread or challah to accompany hearty soups or stews.
4. **Dessert Course**: Enjoy panettone or tsoureki with a cup of coffee or tea.

Bread for a Meaningful New Year

Baking bread for the New Year is more than just a culinary activity—it's a tradition that binds us to cultural heritage and personal intentions for the year ahead. Each loaf carries a story, a hope, or a wish, baked into every crumb. As you prepare these traditional and creative loaves, think of the connections you're fostering and the joy you're sharing. Let this chapter inspire you to break bread with loved ones, symbolizing unity, prosperity, and a fresh start for the year to come.

Chapter 9: Pasta and Noodle Dishes for Longevity

Pasta and noodles have long been associated with prosperity, happiness, and most importantly, longevity. Across cultures, dishes featuring these versatile ingredients symbolize a wish for a long and fulfilling life, making them an ideal addition to your New Year's celebrations. Whether you choose an elegant Italian pasta or a flavorful Asian noodle dish, these meals are rich in tradition, flavor, and meaning.

This chapter will guide you through an array of pasta and noodle recipes, offering global flavors and practical tips to create memorable dishes. Each recipe is designed to delight your guests and add symbolic depth to your New Year feast.

Why Pasta and Noodles for the New Year?

1. **Symbolism of Length**: Long noodles and pasta strands symbolize long life and continuity.
2. **Cultural Traditions**: Many cultures, especially in Asia and Italy, include pasta and noodles in celebrations to express wishes for prosperity and happiness.
3. **Versatility**: Pasta and noodles can be prepared in countless ways, from light and fresh to hearty and comforting.

Tips for Preparing Perfect Pasta and Noodles

1. **Cook to Perfection**: Always cook pasta al dente for a satisfying texture. For noodles, follow package instructions and rinse with cold water if needed to prevent clumping.
2. **Preserve Length**: Avoid cutting noodles to maintain their symbolic meaning.
3. **Choose the Right Sauce**: Pair the dish with a sauce or broth that complements its cultural origin and the ingredients used.
4. **Use Fresh Ingredients**: Fresh vegetables, herbs, and high-quality proteins elevate the flavor and appeal of your dish.

Pasta and Noodle Recipes for Longevity
1. Classic Spaghetti Aglio e Olio (Italy)
A simple yet flavorful dish symbolizing elegance and abundance.

- **Ingredients**: Spaghetti, olive oil, garlic, red chili flakes, parsley, Parmesan cheese.
- **Directions**:
  1. Cook spaghetti until al dente.
  2. Sauté garlic and chili flakes in olive oil. Toss pasta in the oil mixture, garnish with parsley, and serve with grated Parmesan.
  3. **Why It Works**: The simplicity of this dish highlights the purity of its ingredients, making it a timeless classic.

2. Longevity Noodles (China)
A traditional Chinese dish served at celebrations to wish for a long life.

- **Ingredients**: Long wheat noodles, soy sauce, sesame oil, garlic, ginger, green onions, bok choy, shrimp or chicken.
- **Directions**:
  1. Stir-fry garlic, ginger, and protein in sesame oil.
  2. Add cooked noodles, bok choy, and soy sauce. Toss until well combined and garnish with green onions.
  3. **Why It Works**: The long, unbroken noodles are a symbolic wish for unbroken prosperity and happiness.

3. Fettuccine Alfredo with Mushrooms (Italy)
A creamy and indulgent pasta dish perfect for festive occasions.

- **Ingredients**: Fettuccine, heavy cream, Parmesan cheese, garlic, butter, mushrooms, parsley.
- **Directions**:
  1. Cook fettuccine and set aside.
  2. Sauté garlic and mushrooms in butter, then add cream and cheese to create a sauce. Toss pasta in the sauce and garnish with parsley.
  3. **Why It Works**: The rich and creamy sauce adds a luxurious touch to this dish, making it a favorite for celebrations.

4. Japchae (Korea)

A savory-sweet Korean noodle dish made with glass noodles.

- **Ingredients**: Sweet potato starch noodles, spinach, carrots, bell peppers, beef or tofu, soy sauce, sesame oil, sugar, sesame seeds.
- **Directions**:
  1. Cook noodles, rinse with cold water, and set aside.
  2. Stir-fry vegetables and protein, then toss with noodles and a mixture of soy sauce, sesame oil, and sugar. Garnish with sesame seeds.
  3. **Why It Works**: Japchae's vibrant colors and diverse ingredients symbolize harmony and abundance.

5. Pesto Linguine with Pine Nuts (Italy)

A refreshing and aromatic pasta dish ideal for any New Year gathering.

- **Ingredients**: Linguine, basil, garlic, Parmesan cheese, olive oil, pine nuts.
- **Directions**:
  1. Blend basil, garlic, Parmesan, olive oil, and pine nuts into a smooth pesto.
  2. Toss cooked linguine with the pesto and garnish with extra Parmesan and pine nuts.
  3. **Why It Works**: The green color of the pesto symbolizes renewal and health.

6. Pad Thai (Thailand)

A flavorful and balanced noodle dish with tangy and savory notes.

- **Ingredients**: Rice noodles, tamarind paste, fish sauce, palm sugar, eggs, shrimp, tofu, peanuts, bean sprouts, lime.
- **Directions**:
  1. Soak rice noodles in warm water until pliable.
  2. Stir-fry tofu and shrimp, then add noodles and a sauce made from tamarind, fish sauce, and sugar. Garnish with peanuts and lime wedges.
  3. **Why It Works**: The vibrant flavors of Pad Thai make it a festive and crowd-pleasing dish.

7. Ramen Noodle Soup (Japan)

A comforting and hearty soup with long noodles in a flavorful broth.

- **Ingredients**: Ramen noodles, chicken or pork broth, soy sauce, miso paste, boiled eggs, green onions, seaweed, sliced pork or tofu.
- **Directions**:
    1. Simmer broth with soy sauce and miso paste.
    2. Cook noodles and assemble with toppings like boiled eggs, pork, and green onions.
    3. **Why It Works**: Ramen's rich broth and toppings make it a satisfying dish that symbolizes warmth and prosperity.

8. Seafood Linguine (Italy)

A luxurious pasta dish featuring a variety of fresh seafood.

- **Ingredients**: Linguine, shrimp, scallops, mussels, garlic, olive oil, white wine, cherry tomatoes, parsley.
- **Directions**:
    1. Sauté garlic in olive oil, add seafood, and deglaze with white wine.
    2. Toss cooked linguine with the seafood mixture and garnish with parsley.
    3. **Why It Works**: The inclusion of seafood signifies wealth and abundance.

Enhancing Your Pasta and Noodle Dishes

1. **Add Crunch**: Toasted breadcrumbs, crushed nuts, or crispy vegetables can add texture.
2. **Finish with Freshness**: A squeeze of lemon juice, fresh herbs, or a drizzle of olive oil enhances flavor.
3. **Elevate Presentation**: Serve pasta in large bowls or platters with garnishes like edible flowers or microgreens.

Creating a Pasta and Noodle Bar

For a fun and interactive New Year's gathering, set up a DIY pasta and noodle bar:

1. **Base Options**: Offer a variety of noodles and pasta (spaghetti, linguine, rice noodles).
2. **Sauces**: Provide marinara, Alfredo, pesto, and soy-based sauces.
3. **Toppings**: Include proteins (shrimp, chicken, tofu), vegetables, and garnishes (cheese, nuts, herbs).
4. **Presentation**: Use colorful serving dishes and label ingredients for easy customization.

The Legacy of Longevity

Pasta and noodle dishes are more than just delicious—they're steeped in meaning and tradition. Each bite carries a wish for health, happiness, and prosperity. By including these dishes in your New Year's celebration, you're honoring a universal hope for a fulfilling and abundant life. Let these recipes inspire you to create meals that are as rich in flavor as they are in symbolism, ensuring a New Year filled with long-lasting joy.

Chapter 10: Fireworks on the Grill: Barbecued New Year Specials

The sizzle of the grill, the aroma of smoky flavors wafting through the air, and the vibrant energy of the New Year combine to create a perfect setting for barbecued delights. Grilling is not just a cooking method; it's an experience that brings people together, making it a fantastic choice for your New Year's celebration. Whether you're in the heart of winter or enjoying warm weather in a tropical climate, these barbecue recipes will light up your festivities like fireworks.

This chapter is a comprehensive guide to creating show-stopping grilled dishes, from tender meats to flavorful vegetables. We'll explore marinades, grilling techniques, and global flavors to ensure your barbecue menu dazzles your guests and sets the stage for an unforgettable New Year.

Why Barbecue for New Year's?

1. **Festive Atmosphere**: The act of grilling outdoors or even indoors on a stovetop grill brings a lively and communal vibe to the celebration.
2. **Symbolic Fire**: The flames of the grill represent renewal, transformation, and warmth as you transition into the New Year.
3. **Flavor Diversity**: Barbecue techniques, paired with creative marinades and seasonings, offer an array of bold and smoky flavors.

Grilling Essentials
Tools of the Trade:

- **Grill Type**: Choose between a charcoal grill for smoky flavors, a gas grill for convenience, or a stovetop grill for indoor cooking.
- **Tongs and Spatulas**: Long-handled tools are essential for safe and easy flipping.
- **Thermometer**: Ensure meats are cooked to the perfect temperature.
- **Brushes and Skewers**: Use brushes for basting and skewers for kabobs or smaller cuts.

Pro Tips:

1. **Preheat the Grill**: Ensure even cooking by preheating your grill for at least 10 minutes.
2. **Oil the Grates**: Prevent sticking by lightly oiling the grill grates before placing food.
3. **Monitor Heat Zones**: Create direct and indirect heat zones for flexible cooking.
4. **Rest Meats**: Allow grilled meats to rest for 5–10 minutes before slicing to lock in juices.

Barbecue Recipes for a Fiery New Year

1. Honey-Glazed Grilled Chicken

A sweet and smoky favorite that's perfect for all ages.

- **Ingredients**: Chicken thighs, honey, soy sauce, garlic, ginger, smoked paprika.
- **Directions**:
  1. Marinate chicken in a mixture of honey, soy sauce, garlic, ginger, and smoked paprika for at least 2 hours.
  2. Grill over medium heat until cooked through, basting with leftover marinade.
  3. **Pairing**: Serve with coleslaw or a fresh green salad.

2. Herb-Crusted Lamb Chops

An elegant and flavorful dish for a sophisticated barbecue spread.

- **Ingredients**: Lamb chops, rosemary, thyme, garlic, olive oil, lemon zest.
- **Directions**:
  1. Rub lamb chops with a mixture of herbs, garlic, olive oil, and lemon zest.
  2. Grill over high heat for 3–4 minutes per side for medium-rare.
  3. **Pairing**: Serve with mint yogurt sauce or roasted vegetables.

3. Smoky Barbecue Ribs

A crowd-pleaser with tender meat and a sticky glaze.

- **Ingredients**: Pork ribs, barbecue sauce, brown sugar, smoked paprika, garlic powder.
- **Directions**:
  1. Rub ribs with a spice mixture of brown sugar, smoked paprika, and garlic powder.
  2. Slow-cook on indirect heat for 2 hours, then glaze with barbecue sauce and grill for an additional 15 minutes.
  3. **Pairing**: Serve with cornbread and baked beans.

4. Grilled Shrimp Skewers

A quick and flavorful option with a hint of citrus.

- **Ingredients**: Shrimp, garlic, lemon juice, olive oil, chili flakes, parsley.
- **Directions**:
  1. Marinate shrimp in garlic, lemon juice, olive oil, and chili flakes for 30 minutes.
  2. Thread onto skewers and grill over medium heat for 2–3 minutes per side.
  3. **Pairing**: Serve with a citrusy couscous salad.

5. Veggie Kabobs with Balsamic Glaze

A colorful and healthy addition to your barbecue.

- **Ingredients**: Bell peppers, zucchini, mushrooms, red onions, cherry tomatoes, balsamic vinegar, olive oil, thyme.
- **Directions**:
  1. Toss vegetables in a mixture of balsamic vinegar, olive oil, and thyme.
  2. Thread onto skewers and grill until charred and tender.
  3. **Pairing**: Serve with a creamy hummus dip.

6. Cedar-Planked Salmon

Aromatic and moist, this dish is perfect for seafood lovers.

- **Ingredients**: Salmon fillet, maple syrup, Dijon mustard, garlic, cedar plank.
- **Directions**:
  1. Soak the cedar plank in water for at least 2 hours.
  2. Brush salmon with a mixture of maple syrup, Dijon mustard, and garlic, then grill on the cedar plank until cooked through.
  3. **Pairing**: Serve with wild rice and grilled asparagus.

7. Spicy Grilled Pineapple

A sweet and tangy dessert with a hint of heat.

- **Ingredients**: Pineapple rings, brown sugar, cinnamon, cayenne pepper.
- **Directions**:
  1. Sprinkle pineapple rings with brown sugar, cinnamon, and cayenne.
  2. Grill over medium heat for 2 minutes per side until caramelized.
  3. **Pairing**: Serve with vanilla ice cream.

8. Grilled Corn on the Cob with Chili-Lime Butter

A zesty side dish that's a hit with any crowd.

- **Ingredients**: Corn on the cob, butter, lime juice, chili powder, cilantro.
- **Directions**:
  1. Grill corn until charred, then brush with melted butter mixed with lime juice and chili powder.
  2. Sprinkle with chopped cilantro before serving.
  3. **Pairing**: Serve with grilled chicken or ribs.

Global Barbecue Inspiration

1. **Korean Bulgogi (Korea)**: Thinly sliced marinated beef grilled to perfection.
2. **Tandoori Chicken (India)**: Yogurt-marinated chicken with a spicy and smoky flavor.
3. **Argentinian Asado (Argentina)**: A variety of meats grilled with chimichurri sauce.
4. **Jamaican Jerk Chicken (Jamaica)**: Spicy, smoky chicken marinated with jerk seasoning.

Creating a Barbecue Feast

1. **Balance Your Menu**: Include a mix of meats, seafood, vegetables, and a few sweet options.
2. **Set the Scene**: Use string lights, outdoor heaters, or fire pits to create a festive atmosphere.
3. **Interactive Options**: Offer build-your-own kabob stations or DIY taco setups for added fun.
4. **Drink Pairings**: Serve refreshing beverages like sangria, craft beer, or mocktails to complement the smoky flavors.

The Flavor of Fireworks

Grilling for the New Year combines the joy of cooking with the excitement of celebration. Each dish captures the warmth and spirit of the season, from the first sizzle on the grill to the final burst of flavor on the plate. Let these recipes and tips inspire you to create a barbecue menu that will dazzle your guests and light up your New Year with bold, unforgettable flavors. Celebrate with "fireworks on the grill" and start the year with a feast to remember!

Chapter 11: Roasts and Mains to Share with Loved Ones

Roasts and hearty main dishes are the crown jewels of any New Year's feast. They symbolize abundance, warmth, and the joy of togetherness, making them the perfect centerpiece for your celebration. Whether you're hosting an intimate family dinner or a grand gathering with friends, a well-prepared roast or main dish sets the tone for the evening and creates memories that linger well into the New Year.

This chapter dives into the art of preparing roasts and mains that are as flavorful as they are festive. From succulent meats to indulgent vegetarian options, these recipes celebrate the spirit of sharing and the comforting allure of a beautifully presented dish.

Why Roasts and Mains for New Year's?

1. **Symbolism**: Roasts and large mains represent prosperity, abundance, and a year filled with good fortune.
2. **Gathering Point**: A beautifully prepared main dish serves as the focal point of the meal, bringing loved ones together.
3. **Versatility**: With a variety of proteins, vegetables, and seasonings, roasts and mains can be tailored to suit any palate.

Tips for Perfect Roasts and Mains

1. **Choose the Right Cut**: For meats, opt for cuts like prime rib, whole chicken, or pork tenderloin, which are ideal for roasting.
2. **Season Generously**: A flavorful marinade, spice rub, or glaze enhances the dish's taste and aroma.
3. **Low and Slow Cooking**: Roasting at a moderate temperature ensures tender, evenly cooked results.
4. **Rest Before Serving**: Let meats rest for 10–15 minutes after roasting to allow juices to redistribute.

Roast and Main Recipes for New Year's

1. Classic Prime Rib Roast

An indulgent and show-stopping centerpiece that's perfect for the occasion.

- **Ingredients**: Prime rib roast, garlic, rosemary, thyme, olive oil, salt, black pepper.
- **Directions**:
    1. Rub the roast with olive oil, minced garlic, and chopped herbs. Season generously with salt and pepper.
    2. Roast at 450°F (232°C) for 15 minutes, then reduce heat to 325°F (163°C) and cook until the desired doneness (use a meat thermometer for accuracy).
    3. Let rest before slicing and serve with au jus or horseradish sauce.
    4. **Pairing**: Serve with creamy mashed potatoes and roasted vegetables.

2. Herb-Crusted Rack of Lamb

A sophisticated dish with a flavorful herb crust.

- **Ingredients**: Rack of lamb, Dijon mustard, breadcrumbs, parsley, thyme, garlic, olive oil.
- **Directions**:
    1. Rub the lamb with Dijon mustard, then coat with a mixture of breadcrumbs, parsley, thyme, and garlic.
    2. Roast at 400°F (204°C) until the internal temperature reaches 130°F (54°C) for medium-rare.
    3. Let rest and slice into chops for serving.
    4. **Pairing**: Serve with mint jelly and a side of roasted asparagus.

3. Honey-Glazed Ham

A festive and sweet-savory option that's a crowd-pleaser.

- **Ingredients**: Bone-in ham, honey, brown sugar, Dijon mustard, cloves, orange juice.
- **Directions**:
    1. Mix honey, brown sugar, mustard, and orange juice to create a glaze.
    2. Score the ham with a diamond pattern and stud with cloves. Brush with glaze and bake at 325°F (163°C), basting every 30 minutes, until heated through.
    3. **Pairing**: Serve with scalloped potatoes and green beans.

4. Whole Roasted Chicken with Lemon and Herbs

A comforting and versatile dish perfect for sharing.

- **Ingredients**: Whole chicken, lemons, garlic, rosemary, thyme, butter, salt, pepper.
- **Directions**:
    1. Rub the chicken with softened butter and season with salt, pepper, and herbs. Stuff the cavity with lemon halves and garlic cloves.
    2. Roast at 375°F (190°C) until the internal temperature reaches 165°F (74°C).
    3. Let rest before carving.
    4. **Pairing**: Serve with wild rice pilaf and roasted root vegetables.

5. Beef Wellington

A luxurious and impressive dish that will wow your guests.

- **Ingredients**: Beef tenderloin, puff pastry, mushrooms, shallots, Dijon mustard, prosciutto, egg wash.
- **Directions**:
    1. Sear the tenderloin and coat with a mixture of sautéed mushrooms and shallots. Wrap in prosciutto and puff pastry.
    2. Brush with egg wash and bake at 400°F (204°C) until golden and cooked to medium-rare.
    3. **Pairing**: Serve with red wine reduction and buttered green beans.

6. Vegetarian Mushroom and Lentil Loaf

A hearty and flavorful vegetarian option.

- **Ingredients**: Lentils, mushrooms, breadcrumbs, onions, garlic, thyme, tomato paste, soy sauce.
- **Directions**:
    1. Cook lentils and sauté mushrooms, onions, and garlic. Combine with breadcrumbs, tomato paste, soy sauce, and herbs.
    2. Shape into a loaf and bake at 375°F (190°C) until firm.
    3. **Pairing**: Serve with mushroom gravy and mashed sweet potatoes.

7. Porchetta-Style Pork Roast

A crispy and aromatic Italian-inspired dish.

- **Ingredients**: Pork belly, garlic, fennel seeds, rosemary, sage, olive oil, lemon zest.
- **Directions**:
    1. Rub the pork belly with a mixture of garlic, fennel seeds, herbs, and lemon zest. Roll tightly and secure with twine.
    2. Roast at 325°F (163°C) until the internal temperature reaches 145°F (63°C).
    3. **Pairing**: Serve with polenta and sautéed greens.

Enhancing Your Roasts and Mains

1. Glazes and Sauces:

- **Sweet**: Honey-mustard glaze, cranberry reduction.
- **Savory**: Herb butter, red wine jus, mushroom cream sauce.

2. Stuffings:

- Add a flavorful stuffing to your roast, such as wild rice with cranberries or sausage and herb stuffing.

3. Garnishes:

- Fresh herbs, citrus slices, or pomegranate seeds can elevate the presentation.

Serving Suggestions for Roasts

1. **Presentation Matters**: Carve the roast tableside for a dramatic and communal experience.
2. **Side Dish Pairings**: Offer a variety of complementary sides like roasted vegetables, creamy potatoes, and fresh salads.
3. **Wine Pairings**:
    - Red meats: Pair with a bold red wine like Cabernet Sauvignon or Malbec.
    - Poultry: Opt for a lighter red like Pinot Noir or a white wine like Chardonnay.
    - Vegetarian dishes: Complement with a versatile wine like Sauvignon Blanc.

Why Roasts and Mains are Special

Roasts and mains embody the essence of the New Year: warmth, abundance, and the joy of gathering. The act of preparing and sharing these dishes fosters connection, making them a meaningful part of the celebration. Whether you choose a classic roast, an elegant centerpiece, or a hearty vegetarian option, these recipes ensure your New Year feast is one to remember. Celebrate the occasion with love, laughter, and dishes that bring everyone to the table.

Chapter 12: Festive Sides to Complete Your Table

No New Year's feast is complete without an array of delectable side dishes to complement your mains and add variety to your table. Side dishes play a crucial role in enhancing the flavors of the meal, bringing balance, texture, and vibrant colors to your spread. Whether you prefer comforting classics, healthy options, or creative twists, this chapter offers a collection of festive sides that will impress your guests and elevate your celebration.

From creamy gratins to fresh salads and roasted vegetables, these recipes are designed to pair perfectly with roasts, grilled dishes, or vegetarian mains. Each dish celebrates the season's bounty while embodying the warmth and joy of the New Year.

The Importance of Side Dishes

1. **Flavor Balance**: Sides complement and contrast the richness of main dishes, creating a harmonious meal.
2. **Variety**: Offering a mix of textures, colors, and flavors adds interest to the table and ensures there's something for everyone.
3. **Symbolism**: Many sides, such as greens and grains, carry traditional meanings of prosperity, health, and abundance.

Tips for Perfect Sides

1. **Plan Ahead**: Choose sides that can be prepared in advance or require minimal effort on the day of the event.
2. **Seasonal Ingredients**: Use fresh, seasonal produce for the best flavors and textures.
3. **Balance the Menu**: Include a mix of hearty, fresh, and indulgent sides to cater to different tastes.
4. **Presentation**: Serve sides in attractive dishes with garnishes to make them visually appealing.

Festive Side Dish Recipes

1. Creamy Scalloped Potatoes

Rich and indulgent, scalloped potatoes are a timeless favorite.

- **Ingredients**: Potatoes, heavy cream, garlic, Gruyère cheese, thyme, butter.
- **Directions**:
  1. Thinly slice potatoes and layer in a baking dish with minced garlic, cream, and shredded cheese.
  2. Bake at 375°F (190°C) until bubbly and golden on top. Garnish with fresh thyme before serving.
  3. **Pairing**: Perfect with roasts like prime rib or honey-glazed ham.

2. Wild Rice and Cranberry Pilaf

A festive and flavorful grain dish with sweet and savory notes.

- **Ingredients**: Wild rice, dried cranberries, toasted almonds, onions, chicken or vegetable broth, parsley.
- **Directions**:
  1. Cook wild rice in broth with sautéed onions until tender.
  2. Stir in cranberries and almonds, then garnish with parsley before serving.
  3. **Pairing**: Ideal with poultry or vegetarian mains.

3. Roasted Root Vegetables with Maple Glaze

A colorful and earthy dish that's both hearty and healthy.

- **Ingredients**: Carrots, parsnips, sweet potatoes, red onions, olive oil, maple syrup, thyme.
- **Directions**:
  1. Toss vegetables with olive oil, maple syrup, and thyme.
  2. Roast at 400°F (204°C) until caramelized and tender.
  3. **Pairing**: Complements pork or lamb roasts beautifully.

4. Sautéed Green Beans with Garlic and Lemon

Bright and zesty, this dish adds freshness to your table.

- **Ingredients**: Green beans, garlic, olive oil, lemon zest, toasted almonds.
- **Directions**:
  1. Sauté green beans in olive oil with minced garlic until tender-crisp.
  2. Toss with lemon zest and sprinkle with toasted almonds.
  3. **Pairing**: A great match for rich mains like beef Wellington or turkey.

5. Sweet Cornbread with Honey Butter

A Southern-inspired side that's sweet and comforting.

- **Ingredients**: Cornmeal, flour, eggs, buttermilk, honey, butter.
- **Directions**:
    1. Mix ingredients into a batter, pour into a baking pan, and bake until golden.
    2. Serve warm with whipped honey butter.
    3. **Pairing**: Pairs well with barbecue ribs or roasted chicken.

6. Brussels Sprouts with Bacon and Pecans

A savory and slightly nutty dish with a touch of indulgence.

- **Ingredients**: Brussels sprouts, bacon, pecans, olive oil, balsamic glaze.
- **Directions**:
    1. Roast halved Brussels sprouts with olive oil and crumbled bacon.
    2. Toss with toasted pecans and drizzle with balsamic glaze before serving.
    3. **Pairing**: Complements ham or turkey dishes.

7. Citrus and Pomegranate Salad

A refreshing and colorful addition to balance heavier dishes.

- **Ingredients**: Mixed greens, orange segments, pomegranate seeds, red onion, vinaigrette.
- **Directions**:
    1. Toss greens with orange segments, pomegranate seeds, and thinly sliced onion.
    2. Drizzle with a citrus vinaigrette before serving.
    3. **Pairing**: Perfect as a light contrast to rich meats or creamy dishes.

8. Parmesan-Crusted Cauliflower

A crispy and cheesy vegetable dish with a touch of elegance.

- **Ingredients**: Cauliflower florets, Parmesan cheese, breadcrumbs, olive oil, garlic powder.
- **Directions**:
    1. Toss cauliflower with olive oil, then coat in a mixture of Parmesan and breadcrumbs.
    2. Roast at 425°F (218°C) until golden and crispy.
    3. **Pairing**: Pairs wonderfully with seafood or roasted lamb.

9. Buttery Mashed Sweet Potatoes

A creamy and slightly sweet side dish.

- **Ingredients**: Sweet potatoes, butter, cream, maple syrup, cinnamon.
- **Directions**:
  1. Boil sweet potatoes until tender, then mash with butter, cream, and a touch of maple syrup.
  2. Sprinkle with cinnamon before serving.
  3. **Pairing**: Great with pork or turkey.

10. Stuffed Portobello Mushrooms

A hearty and vegetarian-friendly option.

- **Ingredients**: Portobello mushrooms, breadcrumbs, Parmesan cheese, garlic, spinach, olive oil.
- **Directions**:
  1. Remove stems from mushrooms and brush with olive oil.
  2. Fill with a mixture of sautéed spinach, breadcrumbs, and cheese. Bake until golden.
  3. **Pairing**: Serves well alongside roasted chicken or as a standalone option for vegetarian guests.

Creative Twists on Classic Sides

1. **Add International Flavors**: Incorporate spices like cumin, curry powder, or za'atar for a global twist.
2. **Infuse with Herbs**: Use fresh herbs like rosemary, thyme, or dill to add depth to traditional dishes.
3. **Include Textures**: Add crunchy toppings like nuts, seeds, or crispy onions for a delightful contrast.

Serving and Presentation Tips

1. **Coordinate Colors**: Arrange sides to create a visually appealing mix of colors on the table.
2. **Use Elegant Serving Dishes**: Display sides in decorative bowls or platters to elevate the presentation.
3. **Garnish Generously**: Fresh herbs, citrus slices, or a sprinkle of spices add a final touch of sophistication.

Balancing Your New Year's Menu

When planning your sides, consider the main dish and aim for a balance of flavors and textures:

- **With Rich Meats**: Choose lighter sides like salads or green vegetables.
- **With Vegetarian Mains**: Opt for hearty sides like gratins or stuffed vegetables.
- **With Spicy Dishes**: Include cooling sides like creamy mashed potatoes or a citrus salad.

A Feast to Remember

Festive side dishes are the unsung heroes of a New Year's feast. They complete the meal, offering variety, flavor, and visual appeal. By incorporating these recipes into your celebration, you'll create a table that's as beautiful as it is delicious. Let these sides enhance your mains, delight your guests, and contribute to a meal that welcomes the New Year with abundance, joy, and unforgettable flavors.

Chapter 13: Plant-Based New Year Delights

As more people embrace plant-based lifestyles, the New Year is the perfect time to showcase the versatility and richness of plant-based dishes. Whether you're catering to vegans, vegetarians, or simply want to explore creative ways to incorporate more vegetables and plant-based ingredients into your celebration, this chapter offers a wide array of festive recipes. These dishes are flavorful, satisfying, and crafted to impress, ensuring everyone at the table feels included in the celebration.

Why Plant-Based Dishes for the New Year?

1. **Inclusivity**: Plant-based dishes ensure guests with dietary restrictions have delicious options to enjoy.
2. **Symbolism**: Ingredients like greens, grains, and legumes symbolize health, prosperity, and abundance.
3. **Versatility**: Plant-based recipes can range from light and refreshing to hearty and indulgent, catering to all tastes.
4. **Sustainability**: Plant-based cooking supports environmentally conscious dining.

Tips for Creating Plant-Based New Year Dishes

1. **Focus on Flavor**: Use bold seasonings, fresh herbs, and aromatic spices to make dishes vibrant and exciting.
2. **Incorporate Textures**: Combine crunchy, creamy, and tender elements to create satisfying meals.
3. **Highlight Seasonal Produce**: Use fresh, in-season ingredients to maximize flavor and nutritional value.
4. **Think Outside the Box**: Experiment with grains, legumes, and plant-based protein alternatives to add variety.

Plant-Based New Year Recipes
1. Smoky Lentil and Sweet Potato Shepherd's Pie
A comforting, hearty dish with a plant-based twist.

- **Ingredients**: Lentils, sweet potatoes, onions, carrots, celery, garlic, tomato paste, smoked paprika, vegetable broth, olive oil.
- **Directions**:
  1. Sauté onions, carrots, celery, and garlic in olive oil. Add lentils, tomato paste, and smoked paprika, then simmer with vegetable broth until tender.
  2. Mash cooked sweet potatoes with olive oil and seasonings.
  3. Layer lentil mixture in a baking dish, top with mashed sweet potatoes, and bake at 375°F (190°C) until golden.
  4. **Pairing**: Serve with a side of sautéed greens.

2. Mushroom and Spinach Wellington
A plant-based take on a classic, perfect for an elegant main dish.

- **Ingredients**: Puff pastry, mushrooms, spinach, onions, garlic, walnuts, thyme, olive oil.
- **Directions**:
  1. Sauté mushrooms, onions, garlic, and spinach with olive oil and thyme until tender. Chop walnuts and mix into the filling.
  2. Roll out puff pastry, add filling, and fold into a log. Brush with plant-based milk and bake at 400°F (204°C) until golden.
  3. **Pairing**: Serve with vegan gravy or a light salad.

3. Rainbow Quinoa Salad with Citrus Dressing
A vibrant and refreshing dish that symbolizes health and renewal.

- **Ingredients**: Quinoa, red cabbage, bell peppers, carrots, cucumber, parsley, orange juice, olive oil, maple syrup.
- **Directions**:
  1. Cook quinoa and let cool. Toss with shredded vegetables and chopped parsley.
  2. Whisk orange juice, olive oil, and maple syrup for the dressing, and drizzle over the salad.
  3. **Pairing**: Serve as a light starter or a side for heartier mains.

4. Roasted Cauliflower Steaks with Tahini Sauce

A striking and flavorful centerpiece for your plant-based menu.

- **Ingredients**: Cauliflower, olive oil, smoked paprika, garlic powder, tahini, lemon juice, garlic, water.
- **Directions**:
    1. Slice cauliflower into thick "steaks" and brush with olive oil and seasonings. Roast at 425°F (218°C) until golden.
    2. Mix tahini, lemon juice, garlic, and water for the sauce. Drizzle over roasted cauliflower before serving.
    3. **Pairing**: Serve with roasted chickpeas or a side of rice pilaf.

5. Vegan Black-Eyed Pea Gumbo

A hearty and flavorful dish to bring luck and prosperity in the New Year.

- **Ingredients**: Black-eyed peas, okra, onions, bell peppers, celery, garlic, tomatoes, Cajun seasoning, vegetable broth.
- **Directions**:
    1. Sauté onions, peppers, celery, and garlic in olive oil. Add black-eyed peas, okra, tomatoes, and Cajun seasoning.
    2. Simmer with vegetable broth until flavors meld. Serve over rice.
    3. **Pairing**: Complement with cornbread or a green salad.

6. Spaghetti Squash with Garlic and Herb Pesto

A light yet flavorful dish that highlights seasonal produce.

- **Ingredients**: Spaghetti squash, basil, garlic, olive oil, nutritional yeast, walnuts, lemon juice.
- **Directions**:
    1. Roast spaghetti squash until tender, then scrape strands with a fork.
    2. Blend basil, garlic, olive oil, nutritional yeast, walnuts, and lemon juice for the pesto. Toss with the squash and serve.
    3. **Pairing**: Pair with a side of roasted vegetables.

7. Stuffed Bell Peppers with Rice and Beans

A classic comfort food with a healthy, plant-based spin.

- **Ingredients**: Bell peppers, rice, black beans, tomatoes, onions, garlic, cumin, chili powder, nutritional yeast.
- **Directions**:
  1. Hollow out bell peppers and set aside.
  2. Cook rice and mix with black beans, tomatoes, onions, garlic, and spices. Stuff into peppers and bake at 375°F (190°C) until tender.
  3. **Pairing**: Serve with a side of guacamole or salsa.

8. Vegan Spinach Artichoke Dip

A creamy and indulgent appetizer for your New Year's table.

- **Ingredients**: Spinach, artichoke hearts, cashews, nutritional yeast, garlic, lemon juice, plant-based milk.
- **Directions**:
  1. Blend soaked cashews, nutritional yeast, garlic, lemon juice, and plant-based milk into a creamy sauce.
  2. Mix with cooked spinach and artichokes, then bake at 375°F (190°C) until bubbly.
  3. **Pairing**: Serve with pita chips or fresh vegetables.

9. Sweet Potato and Kale Hash

A versatile dish that works as a side or a light main.

- **Ingredients**: Sweet potatoes, kale, onions, garlic, olive oil, smoked paprika.
- **Directions**:
  1. Sauté diced sweet potatoes and onions until golden. Add garlic, kale, and smoked paprika, and cook until kale is wilted.
  2. **Pairing**: Serve with avocado slices or a dollop of plant-based yogurt.

10. Vegan Chocolate Avocado Mousse

A rich and decadent dessert to end your meal on a sweet note.

- **Ingredients**: Avocado, cocoa powder, maple syrup, almond milk, vanilla extract.
- **Directions**:
  1. Blend all ingredients until smooth and creamy.
  2. Chill before serving and garnish with fresh berries or coconut flakes.
  3. **Pairing**: Serve alongside fresh fruit or vegan cookies.

Creating a Plant-Based Feast

1. **Balance the Menu**: Include a mix of hearty mains, fresh sides, and indulgent desserts.
2. **Focus on Presentation**: Use colorful garnishes like pomegranate seeds, fresh herbs, or edible flowers.
3. **Highlight Key Ingredients**: Share the origins and benefits of star ingredients with your guests to create a deeper connection to the meal.

Why Plant-Based Matters

Plant-based New Year dishes celebrate health, sustainability, and inclusivity. They offer an opportunity to explore innovative flavors while honoring traditional values of abundance and prosperity. With these recipes, you'll create a table that's not only delicious but also reflective of the care and thoughtfulness you bring to the New Year. Let these plant-based delights inspire you to embrace a fresh and vibrant start to the year ahead!

Chapter 14: Seafood Spectacular: Ocean-Inspired Dishes

Seafood brings an air of sophistication, freshness, and indulgence to any New Year's celebration. Whether it's succulent shellfish, tender fish, or briny delicacies, ocean-inspired dishes are a timeless choice for festive dining. In many cultures, seafood also holds symbolic meaning, representing prosperity, abundance, and good fortune, making it a fitting addition to your holiday menu.

In this chapter, we'll explore a variety of seafood dishes, from light and refreshing starters to hearty mains. These recipes are designed to showcase the natural flavors of the ocean while incorporating bold seasonings and complementary ingredients. Perfect for intimate dinners or grand gatherings, these dishes will take your New Year's feast to the next level.

Why Seafood for the New Year?

1. **Symbolism**: In many cultures, fish and seafood symbolize wealth and prosperity due to their association with abundance in nature.
2. **Versatility**: Seafood can be prepared in countless ways, from grilling and steaming to frying and baking.
3. **Elegance**: The delicate flavors and textures of seafood elevate any dining experience.
4. **Health Benefits**: Seafood is rich in omega-3 fatty acids, vitamins, and minerals, making it a healthy and nourishing choice.

Tips for Preparing Seafood Dishes

1. **Choose Fresh Seafood**: Fresh, high-quality seafood ensures the best flavor and texture. Look for firm flesh, a clean smell, and clear eyes in fish.
2. **Don't Overcook**: Seafood cooks quickly, so watch your timing to preserve its tenderness.
3. **Enhance, Don't Mask**: Use seasonings and sauces that complement the natural flavors of the seafood rather than overpowering them.
4. **Proper Storage**: Keep seafood refrigerated or on ice until you're ready to cook.

Seafood Recipes for a Spectacular New Year's Feast
1. Classic Shrimp Cocktail
A refreshing and elegant appetizer to start your meal.

- **Ingredients**: Large shrimp, lemon, Old Bay seasoning, cocktail sauce.
- **Directions**:
    1. Boil shrimp with lemon slices and Old Bay seasoning until just cooked.
    2. Chill and serve with a tangy cocktail sauce.
    3. **Pairing**: Serve with champagne or a light white wine.

2. Baked Stuffed Lobster
A luxurious main course that's as impressive as it is delicious.

- **Ingredients**: Whole lobster, breadcrumbs, garlic, parsley, butter, lemon juice.
- **Directions**:
    1. Halve lobsters and remove the meat, leaving the shells intact.
    2. Mix lobster meat with breadcrumbs, garlic, parsley, melted butter, and lemon juice.
    3. Stuff the mixture back into the shells and bake at 375°F (190°C) until golden.
    4. **Pairing**: Serve with garlic butter and a side of roasted potatoes.

3. Seared Scallops with Lemon Butter Sauce
A simple yet elegant dish that highlights the natural sweetness of scallops.

- **Ingredients**: Scallops, butter, garlic, lemon juice, parsley.
- **Directions**:
    1. Pat scallops dry, season, and sear in a hot pan with butter until golden on both sides.
    2. Deglaze the pan with lemon juice and garlic, then drizzle the sauce over the scallops.
    3. **Pairing**: Serve with risotto or a fresh salad.

4. Grilled Salmon with Dill and Mustard Glaze
A flavorful and healthy option for seafood lovers.

- **Ingredients**: Salmon fillets, Dijon mustard, honey, dill, lemon zest.
- **Directions**:
    1. Mix Dijon mustard, honey, dill, and lemon zest to create a glaze.
    2. Brush over salmon fillets and grill until cooked through.
    3. **Pairing**: Serve with steamed asparagus and wild rice.

5. Seafood Paella

A Spanish-inspired dish that's perfect for feeding a crowd.

- **Ingredients**: Arborio rice, shrimp, mussels, clams, chorizo (optional), tomatoes, saffron, garlic, chicken broth.
- **Directions**:
    1. Sauté garlic and onions, then add rice and saffron. Gradually add broth and simmer.
    2. Add seafood and cook until the shells open and the shrimp turn pink.
    3. **Pairing**: Serve with a crisp white wine or sangria.

6. Crispy Fried Calamari

A crunchy and flavorful appetizer that's always a hit.

- **Ingredients**: Calamari rings, flour, cornstarch, paprika, salt, pepper, lemon wedges.
- **Directions**:
    1. Toss calamari in a mixture of flour, cornstarch, paprika, salt, and pepper.
    2. Deep-fry until golden and crispy. Serve with lemon wedges and marinara sauce.
    3. **Pairing**: Complement with a zesty aioli or a cold beer.

7. Steamed Mussels in White Wine Sauce

A light and aromatic dish that's easy to prepare.

- **Ingredients**: Mussels, garlic, shallots, white wine, butter, parsley.
- **Directions**:
    1. Sauté garlic and shallots in butter. Add white wine and bring to a simmer.
    2. Add mussels, cover, and steam until the shells open. Garnish with parsley before serving.
    3. **Pairing**: Serve with crusty bread to soak up the sauce.

8. Crab Cakes with Remoulade Sauce

A deliciously crispy and flavorful seafood treat.

- **Ingredients**: Crab meat, breadcrumbs, egg, mayonnaise, mustard, Old Bay seasoning, parsley.
- **Directions**:
    1. Mix crab meat with breadcrumbs, egg, mayo, mustard, and seasonings. Shape into patties.
    2. Pan-fry until golden and serve with a tangy remoulade sauce.
    3. **Pairing**: Serve with a light salad or coleslaw.

9. Lobster Bisque

A creamy and indulgent soup that's perfect for the New Year.

- **Ingredients**: Lobster shells, heavy cream, tomato paste, garlic, onions, brandy, butter.
- **Directions**:
  1. Sauté lobster shells with garlic and onions. Add tomato paste and brandy, then simmer with broth.
  2. Strain the mixture, stir in cream, and simmer until thickened.
  3. **Pairing**: Serve as a starter with crusty bread.

10. Pan-Roasted Cod with Herb Crust

A light yet satisfying dish with vibrant flavors.

- **Ingredients**: Cod fillets, breadcrumbs, parsley, garlic, lemon zest, olive oil.
- **Directions**:
  1. Mix breadcrumbs, parsley, garlic, and lemon zest. Press onto cod fillets.
  2. Pan-sear until golden, then finish in the oven.
  3. **Pairing**: Serve with roasted vegetables or a quinoa salad.

Enhancing Your Seafood Spread

1. **Fresh Garnishes**: Use lemon wedges, fresh herbs, or edible flowers for a finishing touch.
2. **Themed Presentation**: Serve dishes on nautical-themed platters or with decorative seafood tools.
3. **Sauce Pairings**: Include complementary sauces like garlic butter, remoulade, or cocktail sauce for added flavor.

Pairing Seafood with Drinks

1. **White Wine**: Sauvignon Blanc, Chardonnay, or Pinot Grigio pair beautifully with most seafood.
2. **Sparkling Wine**: Champagne or Prosecco complements the delicate flavors of shrimp, crab, and scallops.
3. **Cocktails**: A classic gin and tonic or a citrusy mojito enhances seafood's freshness.

The Elegance of Ocean-Inspired Dining

Seafood dishes bring a sense of luxury and sophistication to your New Year's table. Each recipe in this chapter celebrates the bounty of the ocean, offering a mix of flavors and textures that cater to diverse palates. Whether you're preparing a casual gathering or an extravagant feast, these ocean-inspired creations will leave your guests with lasting memories of a truly spectacular celebration. Toast to the New Year with the flavors of the sea and start your journey into the year ahead with style and indulgence!

Chapter 15: Sweet Beginnings: Desserts for the New Year

A New Year's celebration isn't complete without a selection of indulgent desserts to end the evening on a sweet note. Desserts symbolize joy, prosperity, and the promise of good things to come, making them an essential part of the festivities. From traditional confections steeped in cultural significance to modern creations that dazzle the senses, this chapter is a feast for the sweet tooth.

We'll explore an array of desserts designed to delight your guests, from elegant pastries to comforting classics. Each recipe is crafted to inspire indulgence, creativity, and celebration, ensuring your New Year's party ends with unforgettable flavors.

Why Desserts for the New Year?

1. **Symbolism**: Desserts often symbolize abundance, good luck, and happiness. Sweet beginnings are believed to set the tone for the year ahead.
2. **Celebratory Nature**: Desserts add an element of festivity and indulgence to any gathering.
3. **Diversity**: With so many flavors, textures, and styles to choose from, there's a dessert to suit every palate.

Tips for Perfect Desserts

1. **Plan Ahead**: Many desserts can be made ahead of time, allowing you to focus on other aspects of your celebration.
2. **Presentation Matters**: Use decorative plates, edible garnishes, and creative plating to make desserts visually appealing.
3. **Balance Flavors**: Offer a mix of rich, creamy, fruity, and light options to cater to diverse preferences.
4. **Portion Wisely**: Small, individual servings allow guests to try multiple desserts without overindulging.

Dessert Recipes for Sweet Beginnings

1. Chocolate Lava Cake

A decadent treat with a molten chocolate center that oozes luxury.

- **Ingredients**: Dark chocolate, butter, eggs, sugar, flour, vanilla extract.
- **Directions**:
    1. Melt chocolate and butter together. Whisk in eggs, sugar, and vanilla, then fold in flour.
    2. Pour into ramekins and bake at 425°F (218°C) until the edges are set but the center is gooey.
    3. **Pairing**: Serve with a scoop of vanilla ice cream or fresh raspberries.

2. Champagne Panna Cotta

An elegant and sparkling dessert perfect for the occasion.

- **Ingredients**: Heavy cream, sugar, gelatin, vanilla, champagne.
- **Directions**:
    1. Heat cream and sugar until dissolved, then add softened gelatin. Stir in champagne and vanilla.
    2. Pour into molds and chill until set.
    3. **Garnish**: Top with gold leaf or fresh berries.

3. Tiramisu

A classic Italian dessert that layers rich flavors of coffee and cream.

- **Ingredients**: Ladyfingers, mascarpone cheese, heavy cream, espresso, cocoa powder, sugar.
- **Directions**:
    1. Dip ladyfingers in espresso and layer with mascarpone cream mixture.
    2. Repeat layers and dust with cocoa powder. Chill for several hours before serving.
    3. **Pairing**: Serve with a glass of espresso martini.

4. Golden Baklava

A crisp and nutty dessert soaked in sweet syrup, symbolizing prosperity.

- **Ingredients**: Phyllo dough, walnuts, pistachios, butter, honey, sugar, cinnamon.
- **Directions**:
    1. Layer phyllo dough with melted butter and a mixture of nuts and cinnamon.
    2. Bake at 350°F (175°C) until golden, then drizzle with a honey-sugar syrup.
    3. **Pairing**: Serve with Turkish coffee or spiced tea.

5. New Year's Eve Trifle

A layered dessert showcasing fruits, cream, and cake for a stunning presentation.

- **Ingredients**: Pound cake, custard, whipped cream, mixed berries, fruit jam.
- **Directions**:
    1. Layer cubes of cake, custard, jam, berries, and whipped cream in a trifle dish.
    2. Repeat layers and garnish with fresh mint and a dusting of powdered sugar.
    3. **Variation**: Use champagne-soaked cake for an added festive touch.

6. Fortune Cookies with Custom Messages

A fun and interactive dessert that adds an element of surprise to the celebration.

- **Ingredients**: Egg whites, sugar, butter, flour, vanilla extract.
- **Directions**:
    1. Mix ingredients into a thin batter. Spread small circles on a baking sheet and bake until edges are golden.
    2. Quickly fold cookies around handwritten fortune strips while still warm.
    3. **Idea**: Include personalized New Year's wishes or predictions.

7. Sparkling Citrus Tart

A refreshing and zesty dessert with a glamorous finish.

- **Ingredients**: Shortbread crust, lemon curd, sugar, eggs, sparkling sugar.
- **Directions**:
    1. Bake a shortbread crust and fill with homemade lemon curd.
    2. Chill until set and sprinkle with sparkling sugar before serving.
    3. **Pairing**: Serve with a sparkling wine.

8. Spiced Pear Crumble

A warm and comforting dessert with seasonal spices.

- **Ingredients**: Pears, brown sugar, cinnamon, nutmeg, oats, butter.
- **Directions**:
    1. Toss sliced pears with sugar and spices. Place in a baking dish and top with a mixture of oats and butter.
    2. Bake at 375°F (190°C) until bubbly and golden.
    3. **Pairing**: Serve with vanilla ice cream or whipped cream.

9. Glittering Macarons

Delicate French cookies with a festive twist.

- **Ingredients**: Almond flour, powdered sugar, egg whites, food coloring, buttercream filling.
- **Directions**:
  1. Whisk egg whites into a meringue, then fold in almond flour and sugar. Pipe into rounds and bake.
  2. Fill with buttercream and decorate with edible glitter.
  3. **Pairing**: Serve with coffee or tea.

10. Midnight Chocolate Bark

A simple, shareable treat with endless customization.

- **Ingredients**: Dark chocolate, white chocolate, nuts, dried fruit, edible gold stars.
- **Directions**:
  1. Melt chocolates separately, spread dark chocolate on a baking sheet, and drizzle with white chocolate.
  2. Swirl with a skewer and top with nuts, fruit, and edible stars. Let set before breaking into pieces.
  3. **Pairing**: Package in small bags for guests to take home.

Dessert Presentation Ideas

1. **Dessert Table**: Create a beautiful dessert station with tiered trays, decorative plates, and signage.
2. **Individual Servings**: Offer mini versions of desserts for easy serving and portion control.
3. **Festive Garnishes**: Use edible flowers, gold leaf, or powdered sugar for an extra touch of elegance.
4. **Interactive Elements**: Include options like build-your-own sundaes or DIY s'mores for added fun.

Sweet Pairings for Desserts

1. **Wine**: Dessert wines like Moscato, Port, or Riesling pair beautifully with most sweets.
2. **Coffee**: Offer espresso, cappuccino, or flavored coffee as an accompaniment.
3. **Cocktails**: Try a creamy Baileys cocktail or a sparkling mimosa to complement your dessert spread.

A Sweet Start to the New Year

Desserts are more than just the final course—they're a way to celebrate life's sweetness and create lasting memories with loved ones. By including these indulgent, elegant, and festive recipes in your New Year's menu, you'll ensure your celebration ends on the highest note. Let these desserts inspire joy and indulgence as you toast to the New Year and all the wonderful moments ahead!

Chapter 16: Gluten-Free and Inclusive Recipes

In today's world, inclusivity is an essential element of any celebration, especially when it comes to food. Accommodating dietary restrictions, such as gluten intolerance or celiac disease, ensures that every guest feels welcome and can enjoy the festivities without worry. This chapter is dedicated to creating an array of flavorful, gluten-free dishes that rival their gluten-containing counterparts, offering options for starters, mains, sides, and desserts.

From using creative alternatives like almond flour, rice flour, and gluten-free oats to employing thoughtful techniques to preserve flavor and texture, these recipes prove that gluten-free doesn't mean flavor-free. With these dishes, you'll craft a menu that everyone, regardless of dietary needs, can savor and celebrate.

Why Gluten-Free and Inclusive Recipes Matter

1. **Inclusivity**: Gluten-free recipes ensure that everyone, including those with gluten sensitivity or celiac disease, can enjoy the meal.
2. **Health-Conscious Choices**: Gluten-free options are often lighter and focus on fresh, wholesome ingredients.
3. **Flavor Innovation**: Using alternative flours and grains opens the door to unique textures and tastes.

Tips for Gluten-Free Cooking and Baking

1. **Use Certified Gluten-Free Ingredients**: Ensure all ingredients, especially flours, oats, and seasonings, are certified gluten-free to avoid cross-contamination.
2. **Experiment with Alternatives**: Almond flour, coconut flour, and gluten-free all-purpose flour blends are excellent substitutes for wheat flour.
3. **Add Structure**: Incorporate binders like xanthan gum or guar gum in gluten-free baking to mimic the elasticity of gluten.
4. **Watch Cross-Contamination**: Use separate utensils, cutting boards, and cookware to prevent contact with gluten-containing foods.

Gluten-Free Recipes for Every Course
Starters and Appetizers
1. Spinach and Artichoke Dip with Gluten-Free Crackers
A creamy and indulgent appetizer that's perfect for sharing.

- **Ingredients**: Spinach, artichoke hearts, cream cheese, Parmesan, garlic, gluten-free crackers.
- **Directions**:
    1. Mix cooked spinach, chopped artichoke hearts, cream cheese, and Parmesan.
    2. Bake at 375°F (190°C) until bubbly and golden. Serve with gluten-free crackers or vegetable sticks.

2. Stuffed Mushrooms with Herbed Quinoa
A savory bite-sized option with a gluten-free filling.

- **Ingredients**: Button mushrooms, cooked quinoa, garlic, parsley, Parmesan.
- **Directions**:
    1. Hollow out mushrooms and stuff with a mixture of quinoa, garlic, parsley, and Parmesan.
    2. Bake at 375°F (190°C) until tender and golden.

Main Dishes
3. Herb-Crusted Chicken with Almond Flour
A crispy and flavorful gluten-free main course.

- **Ingredients**: Chicken breasts, almond flour, garlic powder, paprika, eggs, olive oil.
- **Directions**:
    1. Dip chicken in beaten eggs, then coat in a mixture of almond flour, garlic powder, and paprika.
    2. Pan-fry in olive oil until golden and cooked through.

4. Zucchini Noodles with Pesto and Grilled Shrimp
A light and refreshing gluten-free pasta alternative.

- **Ingredients**: Zucchini, shrimp, basil, garlic, Parmesan, olive oil.
- **Directions**:
    1. Spiralize zucchini into noodles.
    2. Blend basil, garlic, Parmesan, and olive oil for the pesto. Toss noodles with pesto and top with grilled shrimp.

Sides

5. Roasted Sweet Potatoes with Garlic and Rosemary

A hearty and flavorful gluten-free side dish.

- **Ingredients**: Sweet potatoes, garlic, rosemary, olive oil, salt, pepper.
- **Directions**:
    1. Toss cubed sweet potatoes with olive oil, minced garlic, and rosemary.
    2. Roast at 400°F (204°C) until crispy on the outside and tender inside.

6. Wild Rice Pilaf with Cranberries and Almonds

A vibrant, gluten-free grain dish perfect for celebrations.

- **Ingredients**: Wild rice, dried cranberries, toasted almonds, onion, vegetable broth.
- **Directions**:
    1. Sauté onions in olive oil, then add rice and broth. Cook until tender.
    2. Stir in cranberries and almonds before serving.

Desserts

7. Flourless Chocolate Cake

A rich and decadent gluten-free dessert.

- **Ingredients**: Dark chocolate, butter, eggs, sugar, cocoa powder.
- **Directions**:
    1. Melt chocolate and butter together. Whisk in eggs, sugar, and cocoa powder.
    2. Bake at 350°F (175°C) until set. Serve with fresh berries or whipped cream.

8. Gluten-Free Apple Crisp

A comforting and flavorful dessert with a crunchy topping.

- **Ingredients**: Apples, brown sugar, cinnamon, gluten-free oats, almond flour, butter.
- **Directions**:
    1. Toss sliced apples with brown sugar and cinnamon. Place in a baking dish.
    2. Mix oats, almond flour, and butter into a crumbly topping. Spread over apples and bake at 375°F (190°C) until bubbly.

Gluten-Free Bread and Baked Goods
9. Gluten-Free Dinner Rolls
Soft and fluffy rolls that everyone will enjoy.

- **Ingredients**: Gluten-free all-purpose flour, yeast, sugar, eggs, milk, butter.
- **Directions**:
    1. Combine ingredients to form a dough, then let rise until doubled in size.
    2. Shape into rolls and bake at 350°F (175°C) until golden.

10. Almond Flour Biscuits
A savory addition to your gluten-free bread basket.

- **Ingredients**: Almond flour, baking powder, eggs, butter, cheddar cheese.
- **Directions**:
    1. Mix ingredients to form a dough, then shape into biscuits.
    2. Bake at 375°F (190°C) until golden.

Creating a Gluten-Free Feast

1. **Label Clearly**: Indicate which dishes are gluten-free to make it easy for guests to identify their options.
2. **Offer Variety**: Include a mix of mains, sides, and desserts to provide a full, satisfying meal.
3. **Communicate**: Let guests know about your efforts to ensure cross-contamination is avoided for peace of mind.

A Celebration for Everyone
Gluten-free recipes are more than just alternatives—they're an opportunity to create unique and delicious dishes that highlight the versatility of wholesome ingredients. By incorporating these recipes into your New Year's menu, you'll ensure that everyone, regardless of dietary needs, can join in the celebration. Let this chapter inspire you to craft an inclusive feast that's as thoughtful as it is delicious, setting the stage for a New Year filled with unity, health, and joy.

Chapter 17: Family Traditions: Generational Recipes

Family traditions are the cornerstone of New Year's celebrations, often expressed through the time-honored recipes that have been passed down from generation to generation. These dishes carry more than flavor; they are rich with the memories, stories, and love of those who came before us. Preparing and sharing these recipes during the New Year is a way to honor our heritage and create new memories for the next generation.

This chapter delves into the magic of generational recipes, exploring their significance and providing guidance on how to preserve and celebrate these culinary treasures. We'll also share a collection of beloved recipes, each steeped in tradition, to inspire your own family celebration.

Why Generational Recipes Matter

1. **Preserving Heritage**: Recipes passed down through families connect us to our cultural and ancestral roots.
2. **Creating Memories**: Preparing these dishes together fosters connection and creates lasting memories.
3. **Storytelling Through Food**: Every recipe tells a story—of its origins, its creators, and the family moments it has graced.
4. **Continuity and Comfort**: These recipes provide a sense of familiarity and comfort, even as we move into a new year.

How to Preserve Family Recipes

1. **Document the Details**: Write down ingredients, measurements, and step-by-step instructions. Include anecdotes or stories associated with the dish.
2. **Record Cooking Sessions**: Use video or audio recordings to capture the techniques and nuances of preparing the dish.
3. **Create a Family Cookbook**: Compile recipes into a digital or physical book to share with loved ones.
4. **Pass Down Traditions**: Involve younger generations in cooking and teach them the significance of each dish.

Generational Recipes for New Year's
1. Grandma's Pot Roast with Root Vegetables
A comforting classic, slow-cooked to perfection.

- **Ingredients**: Beef chuck roast, carrots, potatoes, onions, garlic, beef broth, thyme, Worcestershire sauce.
- **Directions**:
    1. Sear the roast in a hot skillet until browned.
    2. Place in a slow cooker with vegetables, broth, and seasonings. Cook on low for 8 hours.
    3. **Why It's Special**: Often served at family gatherings, this dish symbolizes warmth and togetherness.

2. Aunt Maria's Tamales
A labor of love and a tradition rooted in family bonding.

- **Ingredients**: Corn masa, pork shoulder, ancho chilies, garlic, lard, corn husks.
- **Directions**:
    1. Prepare masa and slow-cooked pork filling.
    2. Spread masa on soaked corn husks, add filling, and fold. Steam until cooked.
    3. **Why It's Special**: The tamale-making process brings family members together, making it as much about the experience as the food.

3. Nonna's Lasagna
Layered with love, this Italian staple is a generational favorite.

- **Ingredients**: Lasagna noodles, marinara sauce, ricotta cheese, mozzarella, Parmesan, ground beef, garlic, basil.
- **Directions**:
    1. Layer cooked noodles with sauce, cheeses, and beef mixture in a baking dish.
    2. Bake at 375°F (190°C) until bubbly and golden.
    3. **Why It's Special**: A symbol of abundance, this dish often anchors family celebrations.

4. Uncle Joe's Black-Eyed Peas
A Southern tradition for prosperity and luck in the New Year.

- **Ingredients**: Black-eyed peas, ham hock, onions, garlic, celery, chicken broth, bay leaves.
- **Directions**:
    1. Simmer black-eyed peas with ham hock, vegetables, and seasonings until tender.
    2. **Why It's Special**: Believed to bring good luck, this dish is steeped in cultural significance.

5. Nana's Apple Pie

A sweet, flaky dessert that evokes cherished memories.

- **Ingredients**: Granny Smith apples, sugar, cinnamon, nutmeg, butter, flour, shortening, water.
- **Directions**:
    1. Make a flaky crust and fill with spiced apple mixture.
    2. Bake at 375°F (190°C) until the crust is golden and the filling is bubbling.
    3. **Why It's Special**: Often shared during family milestones, this dessert represents love and care.

6. Papa's Pierogi

A Polish classic filled with potatoes and cheese.

- **Ingredients**: Flour, eggs, water, potatoes, cheddar cheese, onions, butter.
- **Directions**:
    1. Prepare dough and roll out circles. Fill with mashed potato and cheese mixture, then seal.
    2. Boil pierogi and sauté in butter with onions.
    3. **Why It's Special**: A dish that bridges generations, bringing family together during its preparation.

7. Great-Grandma's Fruitcake

A recipe steeped in history and holiday tradition.

- **Ingredients**: Dried fruits, nuts, flour, sugar, eggs, butter, rum or brandy.
- **Directions**:
    1. Mix dried fruits and nuts with batter. Bake in a loaf pan and soak with rum.
    2. **Why It's Special**: Passed down over decades, this fruitcake is a testament to resilience and celebration.

8. Mom's Chicken and Dumplings

A hearty, comforting meal perfect for a winter gathering.

- **Ingredients**: Chicken thighs, carrots, celery, onions, flour, baking powder, milk, butter.
- **Directions**:
    1. Simmer chicken and vegetables in broth.
    2. Drop spoonfuls of dumpling dough into the broth and cook until fluffy.
    3. **Why It's Special**: A dish that embodies care and comfort, often prepared during family milestones.

How to Celebrate Generational Recipes

1. **Host a Recipe Day**: Dedicate a day before the New Year for family members to come together and cook these traditional dishes.
2. **Storytelling Over Dinner**: Share stories about the origins of each dish as you enjoy the meal.
3. **Recipe Swap**: Encourage each family member to contribute a recipe and create a shared cookbook.
4. **Teach the Next Generation**: Involve children in the preparation to pass on the skills and traditions.

The Power of Family Traditions

Generational recipes are more than just food—they are a legacy of love, culture, and connection. They remind us of where we come from and provide a sense of continuity as we look toward the future. By honoring these dishes during your New Year's celebration, you'll not only create a feast but also strengthen the bonds that make your family unique. Let these recipes serve as a delicious bridge between the past, present, and future, ensuring that the flavors of tradition continue to thrive for generations to come.

Chapter 18: Spices of the New Year: Infused Recipes

Spices are the heart and soul of cooking, transforming simple ingredients into complex and memorable dishes. They symbolize warmth, excitement, and the promise of new beginnings, making them the perfect centerpiece for your New Year's celebrations. This chapter explores the vibrant world of spices and how you can incorporate them into infused recipes that elevate your holiday table.

From aromatic blends that evoke nostalgia to bold combinations that inspire adventure, these recipes showcase the power of spices to create a feast full of flavor and meaning. Whether you're crafting a savory main, a spiced dessert, or a festive drink, this chapter will guide you through the art of using spices to celebrate the New Year.

Why Spices for the New Year?

1. **Symbolism**: Spices like cinnamon, nutmeg, and saffron are associated with warmth, prosperity, and luxury, making them ideal for celebrating the New Year.
2. **Flavor Enhancement**: Spices add depth and complexity to dishes, elevating even the simplest recipes.
3. **Cultural Significance**: Many spices are tied to traditional New Year's celebrations around the world.
4. **Health Benefits**: Spices like turmeric and ginger are not only flavorful but also known for their health-promoting properties.

Tips for Cooking with Spices

1. **Freshness Matters**: Use fresh, high-quality spices for the best flavor and aroma. Store them in airtight containers away from light and heat.
2. **Toast for Depth**: Toasting whole spices before grinding or using them can unlock their full flavor potential.
3. **Balance Flavors**: Combine spices thoughtfully to balance heat, sweetness, and earthiness.
4. **Start Small**: When trying a new spice or blend, use a small amount and adjust to taste.

Spice-Infused Recipes for the New Year

1. Golden Turmeric Soup

A vibrant and warming starter with immune-boosting properties.

- **Ingredients**: Turmeric, ginger, garlic, coconut milk, vegetable broth, carrots, onions, cilantro.
- **Directions**:
  1. Sauté onions, garlic, and ginger in olive oil. Add turmeric and cook until aromatic.
  2. Stir in carrots, coconut milk, and broth, then simmer until carrots are tender. Blend until smooth.
  3. **Garnish**: Top with a swirl of coconut cream and fresh cilantro.

2. Moroccan-Spiced Lamb Tagine

A rich and aromatic main course inspired by North African flavors.

- **Ingredients**: Lamb, cumin, cinnamon, paprika, coriander, ginger, saffron, chickpeas, dried apricots, almonds.
- **Directions**:
  1. Brown lamb in olive oil, then remove and set aside.
  2. Sauté onions and garlic with spices. Add lamb, chickpeas, apricots, and almonds, then simmer in broth until tender.
  3. **Pairing**: Serve with couscous or flatbread.

3. Chai-Spiced Baked Salmon

A unique take on seafood with warming spices.

- **Ingredients**: Salmon fillets, chai spice blend (cinnamon, cardamom, ginger, cloves), honey, soy sauce.
- **Directions**:
  1. Mix chai spices with honey and soy sauce. Brush over salmon fillets.
  2. Bake at 375°F (190°C) until cooked through.
  3. **Garnish**: Sprinkle with toasted sesame seeds and fresh dill.

4. Garam Masala Roasted Vegetables

A flavorful and colorful side dish.

- **Ingredients**: Sweet potatoes, carrots, cauliflower, garam masala, olive oil, salt, pepper.
- **Directions**:
    1. Toss vegetables with olive oil and garam masala.
    2. Roast at 400°F (204°C) until caramelized and tender.
    3. **Pairing**: Serve with a dollop of spiced yogurt or hummus.

5. Cinnamon-Saffron Rice

A luxurious and fragrant accompaniment to any main dish.

- **Ingredients**: Basmati rice, cinnamon stick, saffron, cardamom pods, butter, slivered almonds.
- **Directions**:
    1. Soak saffron in warm water. Cook rice with cinnamon, cardamom, and saffron water.
    2. Stir in butter and garnish with almonds before serving.
    3. **Pairing**: Complements spiced lamb or roasted chicken.

6. Gingerbread Spiced Cookies

A classic dessert with a festive twist.

- **Ingredients**: Ginger, cinnamon, nutmeg, cloves, molasses, butter, flour, sugar.
- **Directions**:
    1. Cream butter and sugar, then mix in spices and molasses. Add flour and form a dough.
    2. Roll out, cut into shapes, and bake at 350°F (175°C) until golden.
    3. **Garnish**: Decorate with royal icing or powdered sugar.

7. Spiced Mulled Wine

A cozy and aromatic holiday drink.

- **Ingredients**: Red wine, cinnamon sticks, cloves, star anise, orange slices, honey.
- **Directions**:
    1. Simmer wine with spices and orange slices (do not boil).
    2. Sweeten with honey to taste and serve warm.
    3. **Garnish**: Add a cinnamon stick and orange zest for presentation.

8. Cardamom and Rose Panna Cotta

A delicate dessert with floral and spicy notes.

- **Ingredients**: Cream, sugar, gelatin, cardamom pods, rosewater.
- **Directions**:
    1. Heat cream with sugar and crushed cardamom pods. Stir in gelatin and rosewater.
    2. Pour into molds and chill until set.
    3. **Garnish**: Top with crushed pistachios and edible rose petals.

9. Smoked Paprika and Honey Glazed Chicken Wings

A sweet and smoky appetizer perfect for sharing.

- **Ingredients**: Chicken wings, smoked paprika, garlic powder, honey, soy sauce.
- **Directions**:
    1. Toss wings in a mixture of smoked paprika, garlic powder, honey, and soy sauce.
    2. Bake at 400°F (204°C) until crispy.
    3. **Garnish**: Serve with lime wedges and fresh cilantro.

10. Nutmeg-Spiced Hot Chocolate

A comforting drink to end the evening.

- **Ingredients**: Milk, cocoa powder, sugar, nutmeg, cinnamon, whipped cream.
- **Directions**:
    1. Heat milk with cocoa powder, sugar, and a pinch of nutmeg and cinnamon.
    2. Top with whipped cream and a sprinkle of cinnamon.
    3. **Variation**: Add a splash of rum or bourbon for an adult version.

How to Build a Spice-Inspired New Year Feast

1. **Start with Aromatic Starters**: Use warm spices like cumin and coriander in soups or dips.
2. **Highlight a Spiced Main**: Choose bold flavors like garam masala, saffron, or smoked paprika.
3. **Offer Flavorful Sides**: Complement mains with rice, roasted vegetables, or salads infused with spices.
4. **Finish with Spiced Desserts**: Add cinnamon, nutmeg, or cardamom to cookies, cakes, or panna cotta.
5. **Include Spiced Drinks**: Serve mulled wine, chai tea, or spiced hot chocolate for a cozy touch.

The Magic of Spices

Spices hold the power to transform a dish and evoke feelings of warmth, comfort, and celebration. By incorporating these spice-infused recipes into your New Year's feast, you'll create a menu that excites the senses and honors the season's spirit. Let these dishes inspire you to explore new flavors, celebrate tradition, and start the year with bold, unforgettable tastes. Cheers to a flavorful New Year!

Chapter 19: Quick and Easy Recipes for Busy Hosts

Hosting a New Year's celebration is an exciting and joyful experience, but it can also be overwhelming, especially when time is limited. As a host, you want to create a memorable meal that delights your guests, but you don't want to spend the entire day in the kitchen. In this chapter, we will focus on quick, easy, and flavorful recipes that allow you to spend less time preparing and more time enjoying your guests' company.

These recipes are designed to be simple, yet impressive, offering minimal prep and cooking time without sacrificing flavor or presentation. Whether you're preparing appetizers, mains, sides, or desserts, these quick and easy recipes will ensure your celebration is a success without the stress.

Why Quick and Easy Recipes for the New Year?

1. **Save Time**: You'll spend less time cooking and more time with your guests, making the event more enjoyable for everyone.
2. **Stress-Free Entertaining**: When you have a go-to list of easy dishes, hosting becomes fun and relaxed, rather than a chaotic race against time.
3. **Flawless Flavor**: Quick dishes can be just as delicious and impressive as labor-intensive ones, proving that simplicity and flavor can go hand in hand.
4. **Versatility**: These recipes can be adjusted to fit different dietary preferences, making them perfect for inclusive gatherings.

Tips for Hosting with Ease

1. **Prep Ahead**: Many of these recipes can be prepped in advance. Chopping vegetables, making sauces, or marinating meats the night before will save you precious time.
2. **Use Store-Bought Shortcuts**: Don't hesitate to use store-bought ingredients like pre-made doughs, sauces, or frozen vegetables. They'll save time and still taste fantastic.
3. **Set Up a Buffet**: Offer a buffet-style meal, allowing guests to serve themselves and reducing the need for constant attention to plating and serving.
4. **Minimal Equipment**: Choose recipes that require minimal cookware and utensils, so clean-up is quick and easy.

Quick and Easy Recipes for a Stress-Free New Year's Celebration

Appetizers

1. Caprese Skewers

A fresh and simple appetizer that's visually appealing and quick to assemble.

- **Ingredients**: Cherry tomatoes, fresh mozzarella balls, basil leaves, balsamic glaze.
- **Directions**:
    1. Skewer one cherry tomato, one basil leaf, and one mozzarella ball.
    2. Drizzle with balsamic glaze and serve.
    3. **Why It's Easy**: Minimal prep required, no cooking, and a beautiful presentation.

2. Hummus and Veggie Platter

A healthy and crowd-pleasing option.

- **Ingredients**: Store-bought hummus, cucumber, carrots, bell peppers, celery, cherry tomatoes.
- **Directions**:
    1. Arrange fresh veggies around a bowl of hummus.
    2. Serve with pita chips or gluten-free crackers.
    3. **Why It's Easy**: No cooking required, just assembly!

3. Shrimp Cocktail

A classic and elegant appetizer that takes minutes to prepare.

- **Ingredients**: Cooked shrimp, cocktail sauce, lemon wedges.
- **Directions**:
    1. Arrange shrimp on a platter with lemon wedges and cocktail sauce.
    2. **Why It's Easy**: Store-bought shrimp and cocktail sauce make this a breeze.

Mains

4. Sheet Pan Chicken Fajitas

An easy one-pan meal that's both flavorful and customizable.

- **Ingredients**: Chicken breasts, bell peppers, onions, fajita seasoning, olive oil, tortillas.
- **Directions**:
    1. Slice chicken, peppers, and onions, and toss with fajita seasoning and olive oil.
    2. Spread on a sheet pan and bake at 400°F (200°C) for 20-25 minutes.
    3. Serve with warm tortillas and your favorite toppings.
    4. **Why It's Easy**: Quick prep, minimal cleanup, and customizable to your taste.

5. Spaghetti with Garlic and Olive Oil

A light yet satisfying dish that comes together in minutes.

- **Ingredients**: Spaghetti, olive oil, garlic, red pepper flakes, Parmesan.
- **Directions**:
    1. Cook spaghetti according to package instructions.
    2. Sauté garlic in olive oil, add red pepper flakes, and toss with cooked pasta.
    3. Sprinkle with Parmesan and serve.
    4. **Why It's Easy**: Simple ingredients and quick cooking time make this a perfect dish for busy hosts.

6. Quick Stir-Fry Veggies with Tofu

A healthy and flavorful main that's both quick and satisfying.

- **Ingredients**: Tofu, broccoli, bell peppers, carrots, soy sauce, sesame oil, garlic, ginger.
- **Directions**:
    1. Sauté tofu until golden, then remove from the pan.
    2. Stir-fry vegetables with garlic and ginger in sesame oil.
    3. Add tofu back into the pan with soy sauce, cook for another 2 minutes, and serve.
    4. **Why It's Easy**: Minimal prep, quick cooking, and a satisfying plant-based meal.

Sides

7. Roasted Baby Potatoes

A simple side that's full of flavor with just a few ingredients.

- **Ingredients**: Baby potatoes, olive oil, rosemary, garlic, salt, pepper.
- **Directions**:
    1. Toss potatoes with olive oil, rosemary, garlic, salt, and pepper.
    2. Roast at 400°F (200°C) for 20-25 minutes until crispy.
    3. **Why It's Easy**: Quick prep and roasting, with minimal hands-on time.

8. Simple Green Salad with Lemon Vinaigrette

A fresh, light side dish to balance the richness of other dishes.

- **Ingredients**: Mixed greens, cucumber, cherry tomatoes, lemon, olive oil, Dijon mustard, honey.
- **Directions**:
    1. Toss greens with cucumber and cherry tomatoes.
    2. Whisk together lemon juice, olive oil, mustard, honey, salt, and pepper for the dressing.
    3. Drizzle dressing over salad just before serving.
    4. **Why It's Easy**: Fast, healthy, and refreshing.

Desserts

9. No-Bake Cheesecake Cups

An easy dessert with minimal effort and a show-stopping look.

- **Ingredients**: Cream cheese, powdered sugar, vanilla, graham cracker crumbs, butter, fresh berries.
- **Directions**:
    1. Combine cream cheese, powdered sugar, and vanilla.
    2. Layer graham cracker crumbs and cheesecake mixture in small cups.
    3. Top with fresh berries and refrigerate until ready to serve.
    4. **Why It's Easy**: No baking, just assembling, and a perfect make-ahead treat.

10. Chocolate-Dipped Strawberries

A simple, elegant dessert that requires no baking.

- **Ingredients**: Fresh strawberries, dark or milk chocolate, white chocolate for drizzling.
- **Directions**:
    1. Melt the dark or milk chocolate and dip strawberries in it.
    2. Drizzle with melted white chocolate for a decorative touch.
    3. Let set on parchment paper.
    4. **Why It's Easy**: Quick to prepare and looks fancy with minimal effort.

Entertaining Tips for Busy Hosts

1. **Make-Ahead Dishes**: Choose recipes that can be made in advance, such as dips, salads, or marinated meats, so you can focus on other aspects of the party.
2. **Keep It Simple**: Don't feel the need to make every dish elaborate. Sometimes, a simple recipe done well is all you need.
3. **Set a Buffet**: Let guests serve themselves from a buffet-style table, which reduces your workload and allows everyone to enjoy a variety of dishes.
4. **Involve Guests**: Set up a DIY taco bar, salad station, or dessert station, where guests can customize their meals or treats.

A Stress-Free, Delicious Celebration

With these quick and easy recipes, you can host a beautiful, delicious, and memorable New Year's celebration without the stress of hours spent in the kitchen. Each dish is designed to be simple, yet impressive, so you can enjoy the company of your guests while still serving a spread that will leave everyone satisfied. Whether you're preparing appetizers, mains, sides, or desserts, these recipes will help you throw a spectacular celebration with ease.

Chapter 20: Make-Ahead Dishes for a Stress-Free New Year

The secret to hosting a seamless and enjoyable New Year's celebration lies in preparation. Make-ahead dishes allow you to minimize last-minute stress while still offering your guests a delicious and impressive spread. These recipes are designed to be prepped in advance, giving you more time to focus on entertaining, decorating, or simply enjoying the festivities with your loved ones.

This chapter highlights a range of appetizers, mains, sides, and desserts that can be prepared ahead of time, stored, and reheated or assembled just before serving. With these make-ahead dishes, you can create a stress-free celebration that's as enjoyable for you as it is for your guests.

Why Make-Ahead Dishes?

1. **Time Management**: Prepping in advance frees up time on the day of the event, allowing you to focus on other tasks.
2. **Reduced Stress**: You'll feel more relaxed knowing that the bulk of the cooking is already done.
3. **Improved Flavor**: Many dishes, like stews and marinated proteins, taste better after resting as flavors meld together.
4. **More Time with Guests**: Spend less time in the kitchen and more time celebrating with your friends and family.

Tips for Make-Ahead Success

1. **Choose Dishes Wisely**: Opt for recipes that store and reheat well, such as casseroles, soups, and baked goods.
2. **Proper Storage**: Use airtight containers, plastic wrap, or foil to preserve freshness and flavor.
3. **Label Clearly**: Label containers with the contents and reheating instructions to avoid confusion.
4. **Reheat Gently**: Warm dishes on low heat to preserve texture and prevent overcooking.
5. **Plan Serving Timing**: Make a schedule for when dishes need to be reheated or assembled.

Make-Ahead Recipes for the New Year
Appetizers
1. Spinach and Feta Phyllo Triangles
A crowd-pleasing finger food that's easy to prepare in advance.

- **Ingredients**: Phyllo dough, spinach, feta cheese, onions, garlic, olive oil, butter.
- **Directions**:
    1. Sauté spinach, onions, and garlic, then mix with crumbled feta.
    2. Fill phyllo dough, fold into triangles, and brush with butter. Freeze or refrigerate until needed.
    3. Bake at 375°F (190°C) just before serving.
    4. **Storage**: Can be frozen for up to a month.

2. Deviled Eggs
A classic appetizer that can be made ahead and assembled later.

- **Ingredients**: Hard-boiled eggs, mayonnaise, Dijon mustard, paprika.
- **Directions**:
    1. Prepare the filling and store in a piping bag.
    2. Halve boiled eggs and refrigerate separately.
    3. Pipe filling into egg whites just before serving.
    4. **Storage**: Keep refrigerated for up to 2 days.

Main Dishes
3. Beef Bourguignon
A rich, flavorful dish that improves with time.

- **Ingredients**: Beef chuck, red wine, beef broth, carrots, onions, mushrooms, garlic, thyme, bacon.
- **Directions**:
    1. Sear beef and cook with wine, broth, vegetables, and herbs until tender.
    2. Refrigerate and reheat gently on the stove or in a slow cooker.
    3. **Storage**: Store in an airtight container for up to 3 days.

4. Chicken Enchiladas

A hearty and customizable make-ahead main.

- **Ingredients**: Tortillas, shredded chicken, enchilada sauce, cheese, onions, cilantro.
- **Directions**:
    1. Assemble enchiladas in a baking dish and cover with sauce and cheese.
    2. Refrigerate or freeze. Bake at 375°F (190°C) until bubbly before serving.
    3. **Storage**: Freeze for up to 2 months.

Sides

5. Potato Gratin

A creamy and indulgent side that reheats beautifully.

- **Ingredients**: Potatoes, heavy cream, garlic, Gruyère cheese, nutmeg.
- **Directions**:
    1. Layer sliced potatoes with cream, garlic, and cheese in a baking dish.
    2. Bake partially, then refrigerate. Finish baking on the day of the event.
    3. **Storage**: Refrigerate for up to 2 days.

6. Wild Rice and Cranberry Salad

A fresh and tangy side dish that holds up well.

- **Ingredients**: Wild rice, dried cranberries, toasted almonds, green onions, vinaigrette.
- **Directions**:
    1. Cook rice and mix with cranberries, almonds, and onions.
    2. Toss with vinaigrette and store in the fridge. Serve cold or at room temperature.
    3. **Storage**: Refrigerate for up to 3 days.

Desserts

7. Tiramisu

A no-bake dessert that tastes even better after a day or two in the fridge.

- **Ingredients**: Ladyfingers, mascarpone cheese, espresso, cocoa powder, sugar, heavy cream.
- **Directions**:
    1. Layer ladyfingers soaked in espresso with mascarpone cream.
    2. Chill for at least 6 hours or overnight. Dust with cocoa powder before serving.
    3. **Storage**: Refrigerate for up to 3 days.

8. Chocolate Mousse

A decadent dessert that can be made well in advance.

- **Ingredients**: Dark chocolate, eggs, sugar, heavy cream.
- **Directions**:
    1. Whip cream and fold into melted chocolate and egg mixture.
    2. Portion into cups and chill until ready to serve.
    3. **Storage**: Refrigerate for up to 2 days.

Drinks

9. Spiced Mulled Cider

A warming beverage that can be prepared ahead and reheated.

- **Ingredients**: Apple cider, cinnamon sticks, cloves, star anise, orange slices.
- **Directions**:
    1. Simmer all ingredients and strain. Store in a pitcher and reheat on the stove or slow cooker.
    2. **Storage**: Refrigerate for up to 3 days.

10. Sangria

A festive drink that benefits from being made ahead.

- **Ingredients**: Red wine, orange juice, brandy, sliced fruits (oranges, lemons, berries).
- **Directions**:
    1. Combine all ingredients in a large pitcher and chill for at least 4 hours.
    2. **Storage**: Refrigerate for up to 2 days.

The Make-Ahead Hosting Schedule

1. **2 Days Before**: Prepare soups, stews, and desserts like tiramisu or mousse.
2. **1 Day Before**: Assemble casseroles, gratins, and enchiladas. Chop vegetables and prepare salads.
3. **Morning of the Event**: Reheat mains, bake partially prepped dishes, and assemble appetizers.
4. **Just Before Serving**: Finish plating salads, warm bread, and garnish dishes.

The Ease of Make-Ahead Magic

Make-ahead dishes are the ultimate hosting hack, allowing you to create a feast that's as impressive as it is stress-free. With thoughtful preparation, you can offer a menu that's flavorful, beautifully presented, and easy to manage. These recipes and tips will ensure your New Year's celebration is a joyful, delicious experience for you and your guests. Here's to a stress-free start to the New Year!

Chapter 21: Holiday Breakfasts to Start the Year Energized

The first breakfast of the New Year is a meaningful way to set the tone for the days ahead. It's a time to gather with loved ones, reflect on new beginnings, and enjoy a hearty, energizing meal that fuels the day. Whether you're hosting a relaxed brunch or treating yourself to a quiet morning, the right breakfast can be a comforting and celebratory experience.

In this chapter, we explore a variety of holiday breakfasts designed to kick off the year with flavor, nourishment, and joy. From classic comfort foods to elegant brunch options, these recipes are perfect for starting the New Year on a delicious and energizing note.

Why a Special Holiday Breakfast?

1. **Celebration of New Beginnings**: A festive breakfast symbolizes renewal and optimism for the year ahead.
2. **Connection**: Gathering for breakfast creates an intimate setting to spend time with loved ones after the excitement of New Year's Eve.
3. **Fuel for the Day**: A hearty and nutritious breakfast provides the energy needed to embrace the opportunities of a fresh year.
4. **Tradition Building**: Creating a special New Year's breakfast can become a cherished family ritual.

Tips for Crafting the Perfect Holiday Breakfast

1. **Balance Flavors and Textures**: Include a mix of sweet, savory, light, and hearty options to cater to all preferences.
2. **Prepare Ahead**: Choose recipes that allow for some prep work the night before, so the morning is stress-free.
3. **Use Seasonal Ingredients**: Highlight winter produce like citrus, pomegranate, and hearty greens for freshness and vibrancy.
4. **Create a Cozy Atmosphere**: Use festive table settings, soft lighting, and a warm drink station to make breakfast feel special.

Holiday Breakfast Recipes for the New Year
Sweet Options
1. Citrus Ricotta Pancakes
Fluffy pancakes with a hint of citrus brightness.

- **Ingredients**: Ricotta cheese, flour, eggs, sugar, lemon zest, orange zest, baking powder, milk.
- **Directions**:
  1. Whisk ricotta, eggs, sugar, milk, and citrus zest. Gradually add dry ingredients and mix until smooth.
  2. Cook on a griddle until golden on both sides.
  3. Serve with powdered sugar, maple syrup, or a citrus compote.
  4. **Why It's Energizing**: The zesty flavors and protein-rich ricotta provide a refreshing and satisfying start.

2. Overnight Cinnamon Roll Casserole
A decadent dish that's easy to prepare in advance.

- **Ingredients**: Pre-made cinnamon rolls, eggs, milk, vanilla extract, cinnamon, powdered sugar.
- **Directions**:
  1. Cut cinnamon rolls into pieces and place in a greased baking dish.
  2. Mix eggs, milk, vanilla, and cinnamon, then pour over the rolls. Cover and refrigerate overnight.
  3. Bake at 350°F (175°C) in the morning, then drizzle with icing.
  4. **Why It's Perfect**: Sweet and indulgent, it's a treat that feels festive and effortless.

3. Pomegranate and Yogurt Parfaits
A light and colorful option packed with antioxidants.

- **Ingredients**: Greek yogurt, granola, pomegranate seeds, honey, mint leaves.
- **Directions**:
  1. Layer yogurt, granola, and pomegranate seeds in a glass. Drizzle with honey and garnish with mint.
  2. **Why It's Energizing**: The yogurt provides protein, and pomegranate seeds add a burst of freshness.

Savory Options

4. Breakfast Strata with Spinach and Gruyère

A savory egg-based casserole that's loaded with flavor.

- **Ingredients**: Bread cubes, eggs, milk, spinach, Gruyère cheese, onions, garlic, thyme.
- **Directions**:
  1. Sauté onions, garlic, and spinach. Layer bread cubes in a baking dish and top with the sautéed mixture and cheese.
  2. Whisk eggs, milk, and seasonings, then pour over the bread. Cover and refrigerate overnight.
  3. Bake at 350°F (175°C) until golden and set.
  4. **Why It's Perfect**: This make-ahead dish is hearty, cheesy, and packed with nutrients.

5. Smoked Salmon Bagel Bar

An interactive and elegant breakfast option.

- **Ingredients**: Bagels, cream cheese, smoked salmon, capers, red onions, cucumbers, dill.
- **Directions**:
  1. Set up a bagel bar with sliced bagels, spreads, and toppings for guests to customize.
  2. **Why It's Energizing**: Protein from the salmon and cream cheese keeps you satisfied, while the variety of toppings makes it fun and personalized.

6. Shakshuka (Poached Eggs in Spiced Tomato Sauce)

A flavorful and warming Middle Eastern-inspired dish.

- **Ingredients**: Eggs, tomatoes, onions, garlic, bell peppers, paprika, cumin, chili flakes, parsley.
- **Directions**:
  1. Sauté onions, garlic, and bell peppers with spices. Add tomatoes and simmer until thickened.
  2. Make small wells in the sauce and crack eggs into them. Cover and cook until eggs are set.
  3. Garnish with parsley and serve with crusty bread.
  4. **Why It's Perfect**: Packed with protein and bold flavors, it's a vibrant way to start the year.

Drinks

7. Freshly Squeezed Citrus Juice

A refreshing and vitamin-packed beverage.

- **Ingredients**: Oranges, grapefruits, lemons, limes, honey (optional).
- **Directions**:
    1. Juice a combination of citrus fruits and sweeten with honey if desired. Serve chilled.
    2. **Why It's Energizing**: High in vitamin C, this drink boosts immunity and refreshes the palate.

8. Spiced Chai Latte

A cozy and aromatic drink to accompany breakfast.

- **Ingredients**: Black tea, milk, cinnamon, cardamom, cloves, ginger, sugar.
- **Directions**:
    1. Simmer tea with spices and sweeten with sugar. Add milk and heat until frothy.
    2. **Why It's Energizing**: The warming spices and gentle caffeine provide a comforting energy boost.

Baked Goods

9. Savory Cheddar and Herb Scones

Flaky and flavorful scones that pair well with savory dishes.

- **Ingredients**: Flour, baking powder, butter, cheddar cheese, chives, milk.
- **Directions**:
    1. Mix dry ingredients with butter until crumbly. Add cheese, chives, and milk to form a dough.
    2. Cut into wedges and bake at 375°F (190°C) until golden.
    3. **Why It's Perfect**: A versatile option that's easy to make ahead and reheat.

10. Banana Oat Muffins

A healthy and portable breakfast option.

- **Ingredients**: Bananas, oats, eggs, honey, baking powder, cinnamon.
- **Directions**:
    1. Blend ingredients into a smooth batter, pour into muffin tins, and bake at 350°F (175°C).
    2. **Why It's Energizing**: The oats provide long-lasting energy, and the bananas add natural sweetness.

Crafting a Memorable Holiday Breakfast

1. **Set the Scene**: Create a warm and inviting atmosphere with candles, table runners, and festive dishes.
2. **Serve Family Style**: Lay out dishes on the table for easy sharing and a relaxed vibe.
3. **Offer Variety**: Include both sweet and savory options to cater to all preferences.
4. **Add a Personal Touch**: Include a dish that reflects your family's traditions or favorite flavors.

A Delicious Start to the New Year

Starting the year with a festive and nourishing breakfast is more than just a meal—it's a celebration of hope, connection, and joy. These holiday breakfast recipes are designed to energize your day and bring loved ones together in the spirit of renewal. Whether you prefer sweet indulgences, savory comforts, or a mix of both, this chapter offers the perfect recipes to help you start the year on a delicious and memorable note. Here's to a bright and flavorful New Year!

Chapter 22: Beverage Creations: Mocktails and Mixology

A New Year's celebration is never complete without a selection of drinks that delight the senses and keep the festivities lively. Whether you're raising a glass to toast the New Year or offering refreshing options for non-drinkers, creating beverages with flair is a wonderful way to elevate the experience. Mocktails (non-alcoholic cocktails) and mixology (the art of crafting cocktails) allow you to showcase creativity and serve drinks that complement your menu and wow your guests.

This chapter explores the world of beverage creations, offering a mix of non-alcoholic and alcoholic recipes that balance flavor, presentation, and ease of preparation. These drinks range from sophisticated to playful, ensuring there's something for everyone to enjoy.

Why Beverage Creations for the New Year?

1. **Celebratory Atmosphere**: Signature drinks add an element of fun and sophistication to the festivities.
2. **Inclusivity**: Mocktails ensure that non-drinkers, designated drivers, and younger guests feel included in the celebration.
3. **Customization**: Drinks can be tailored to suit personal tastes, themes, and dietary preferences.
4. **Visual Appeal**: Vibrant colors, garnishes, and glassware create an Instagram-worthy drink station.

Tips for Beverage Success

1. **Balance Flavors**: Aim for a mix of sweet, sour, bitter, and savory notes to create well-rounded drinks.
2. **Use Fresh Ingredients**: Fresh fruits, herbs, and juices make a noticeable difference in flavor and presentation.
3. **Garnish with Care**: A simple garnish, such as citrus slices, fresh herbs, or edible flowers, can elevate a drink's appearance.
4. **Offer Variety**: Include options for mocktails, cocktails, and customizable bases to accommodate all preferences.
5. **Prepare in Batches**: For larger gatherings, prepare big-batch drinks or punch bowls to minimize individual mixing.

Mocktail Recipes

1. Sparkling Citrus Punch

A bubbly, citrusy drink that's perfect for toasting.

- **Ingredients**: Orange juice, lemon juice, sparkling water, grenadine, orange slices, fresh mint.
- **Directions**:
    1. Mix orange and lemon juice in a pitcher.
    2. Pour into glasses, top with sparkling water, and add a splash of grenadine.
    3. Garnish with orange slices and mint.
    4. **Why It's Special**: Vibrant and refreshing, this drink is a crowd-pleaser for all ages.

2. Cucumber and Lime Cooler

A crisp and hydrating mocktail with a touch of sweetness.

- **Ingredients**: Cucumber slices, lime juice, simple syrup, soda water, fresh mint.
- **Directions**:
    1. Muddle cucumber slices and mint in a shaker.
    2. Add lime juice, simple syrup, and ice. Shake well.
    3. Strain into a glass over ice and top with soda water.
    4. **Why It's Special**: Light and cooling, this is ideal for a post-party refresh.

3. Pomegranate Sparkler

A ruby-red drink with tangy and sweet notes.

- **Ingredients**: Pomegranate juice, cranberry juice, sparkling apple cider, pomegranate seeds, rosemary sprigs.
- **Directions**:
    1. Mix pomegranate and cranberry juice in a glass.
    2. Top with sparkling apple cider.
    3. Garnish with pomegranate seeds and a rosemary sprig.
    4. **Why It's Special**: The festive color and garnish make it perfect for a New Year's toast.

4. Virgin Piña Colada

A tropical treat that brings the sunshine to your table.

- **Ingredients**: Pineapple juice, coconut cream, ice, maraschino cherry.
- **Directions**:
    1. Blend pineapple juice, coconut cream, and ice until smooth.
    2. Pour into a glass and garnish with a cherry.
    3. **Why It's Special**: Creamy and sweet, it's a vacation in a glass.

5. Ginger Basil Lemonade
A refreshing twist on a classic.

- **Ingredients**: Fresh basil leaves, ginger syrup, lemon juice, water, lemon slices.
- **Directions**:
  1. Muddle basil leaves with ginger syrup in a shaker.
  2. Add lemon juice and water. Shake well and strain into a glass.
  3. Garnish with lemon slices and a basil leaf.
  4. **Why It's Special**: The ginger adds a spicy kick, balancing the sweetness.

Cocktail Recipes
6. Classic Champagne Cocktail
A simple yet elegant toast to the New Year.

- **Ingredients**: Champagne, sugar cube, Angostura bitters, lemon twist.
- **Directions**:
    1. Place a sugar cube in a champagne flute and add a few dashes of bitters.
    2. Fill the flute with champagne and garnish with a lemon twist.
    3. **Why It's Special**: Timeless and celebratory, this cocktail is perfect for a midnight toast.

7. Spicy Margarita
A zesty drink with a hint of heat.

- **Ingredients**: Tequila, lime juice, triple sec, simple syrup, jalapeño slices, salt.
- **Directions**:
    1. Rim a glass with salt and jalapeño slices.
    2. Shake tequila, lime juice, triple sec, and simple syrup with ice.
    3. Strain into the prepared glass over ice.
    4. **Why It's Special**: The spicy kick makes this margarita unforgettable.

8. Espresso Martini
A sophisticated cocktail with a caffeine boost.

- **Ingredients**: Vodka, espresso, coffee liqueur, simple syrup.
- **Directions**:
    1. Shake vodka, espresso, coffee liqueur, and simple syrup with ice.
    2. Strain into a martini glass and garnish with coffee beans.
    3. **Why It's Special**: Rich and smooth, it's an ideal pick-me-up.

9. Mojito Royale
A sparkling twist on the classic mojito.

- **Ingredients**: White rum, lime juice, sugar, mint leaves, sparkling wine.
- **Directions**:
    1. Muddle mint leaves, sugar, and lime juice in a glass.
    2. Add rum and top with sparkling wine.
    3. Garnish with a mint sprig.
    4. **Why It's Special**: The addition of sparkling wine elevates the classic mojito.

10. Winter Sangria

A warm, spiced take on sangria.

- **Ingredients**: Red wine, brandy, orange juice, cinnamon sticks, cloves, sliced oranges and apples.
- **Directions**:
    1. Mix all ingredients in a large pitcher and let sit for at least 4 hours.
    2. Serve over ice with fruit slices.
    3. **Why It's Special**: The warming spices and bold flavors make it a perfect winter drink.

Presentation Tips for Drinks

1. **Glassware Matters**: Use appropriate glasses (e.g., flutes, highballs, or martini glasses) to enhance the drink's appeal.
2. **Garnishes**: Fresh herbs, fruit slices, edible flowers, or sugared rims add visual interest.
3. **Color Coordination**: Serve drinks that complement the overall color scheme of your event.
4. **Drink Station**: Set up a self-serve station with mixers, garnishes, and labeled recipes for guests to mix their own drinks.

Crafting the Perfect Drink Menu

1. **Offer Variety**: Include both mocktails and cocktails to cater to all preferences.
2. **Match the Menu**: Choose drinks that pair well with the food you're serving.
3. **Seasonal Ingredients**: Incorporate winter fruits and spices like pomegranate, citrus, ginger, and cinnamon for a festive touch.
4. **Prepare for the Toast**: Have glasses ready for a midnight toast with champagne or a sparkling mocktail.

A Toast to the New Year

Whether you're crafting elegant cocktails or refreshing mocktails, these beverage creations bring joy, sophistication, and a sense of celebration to your New Year's event. With thoughtful combinations of flavors and eye-catching presentation, these drinks will elevate your party and leave a lasting impression on your guests. Cheers to the New Year and all the delightful moments ahead!

Chapter 23: Festive Fusion: Blending Cultures in Recipes

The New Year is a global celebration, with unique traditions and flavors spanning cultures worldwide. Fusion cuisine offers the perfect opportunity to honor these diverse traditions by blending ingredients, techniques, and flavors from different cultures to create something new, exciting, and meaningful. By exploring fusion recipes, you can craft a festive menu that celebrates inclusivity, creativity, and the joy of shared experiences.

In this chapter, we explore a variety of fusion recipes that seamlessly combine elements from different culinary traditions. These dishes, drinks, and desserts are not only delicious but also carry the spirit of unity and celebration, making them perfect for your New Year's festivities.

Why Festive Fusion?

1. **Cultural Appreciation**: Fusion recipes honor and celebrate global traditions by incorporating elements from various cuisines.
2. **Creativity**: The blending of ingredients and techniques allows for innovative and surprising flavor combinations.
3. **Inclusivity**: Fusion dishes appeal to a wide range of palates, ensuring there's something for everyone.
4. **Memorable Dining**: Unique and unexpected pairings make your celebration stand out and leave a lasting impression on guests.

Tips for Creating Fusion Recipes

1. **Start with Familiar Flavors**: Begin with a dish or ingredient you know well and introduce elements from another cuisine.
2. **Balance is Key**: Ensure that the flavors complement rather than overpower one another.
3. **Respect Tradition**: Understand the cultural significance of ingredients and techniques to maintain authenticity while blending cuisines.
4. **Experiment Mindfully**: Test small batches of recipes to fine-tune flavors and textures before serving them to guests.

Fusion Recipes for Your Festive Menu
Appetizers
1. Sushi Tacos
A playful combination of Japanese sushi and Mexican tacos.

- **Ingredients**: Sushi rice, nori sheets, avocado, raw fish (tuna or salmon), soy sauce, wasabi, lime juice.
- **Directions**:
  1. Cut nori sheets into small taco-sized pieces and shape into taco shells.
  2. Fill with sushi rice, raw fish, avocado, and a drizzle of soy sauce mixed with lime juice.
  3. Garnish with sesame seeds and wasabi mayo.
  4. **Why It Works**: The freshness of sushi meets the fun and portability of tacos.

2. Kimchi Quesadillas
A spicy, cheesy blend of Korean and Mexican flavors.

- **Ingredients**: Tortillas, kimchi, shredded cheese (cheddar or mozzarella), green onions, sesame oil.
- **Directions**:
  1. Spread kimchi on one side of a tortilla, sprinkle with cheese and green onions, and top with another tortilla.
  2. Cook in a skillet with sesame oil until golden and crispy.
  3. Slice into wedges and serve with sour cream or sriracha mayo.
  4. **Why It Works**: The tangy heat of kimchi pairs beautifully with melted cheese.

Main Dishes

3. Tandoori Chicken Pizza

A spicy, aromatic take on pizza with Indian influences.

- **Ingredients**: Pizza dough, tandoori-marinated chicken, tomato sauce, mozzarella, red onions, cilantro.
- **Directions**:
  1. Spread tomato sauce on pizza dough, add marinated chicken, onions, and cheese.
  2. Bake at 450°F (232°C) until the crust is crispy and the cheese is melted.
  3. Garnish with fresh cilantro before serving.
  4. **Why It Works**: The bold spices of tandoori chicken bring a unique twist to a classic dish.

4. Bulgogi Beef Tacos

Korean BBQ flavors meet the simplicity of tacos.

- **Ingredients**: Thinly sliced beef (bulgogi), soy sauce, sugar, garlic, sesame oil, tortillas, slaw (cabbage, carrots), sriracha mayo.
- **Directions**:
  1. Marinate beef in a bulgogi sauce mixture and cook until caramelized.
  2. Fill tortillas with beef and slaw, and drizzle with sriracha mayo.
  3. **Why It Works**: The sweet and savory flavors of bulgogi complement the crunch of fresh slaw.

Sides

5. Mediterranean Spring Rolls

A fresh, handheld fusion of Vietnamese and Mediterranean cuisines.

- **Ingredients**: Rice paper wrappers, hummus, tabbouleh, feta cheese, cucumber, mint.
- **Directions**:
    1. Soak rice paper wrappers until pliable.
    2. Fill with hummus, tabbouleh, feta, cucumber slices, and fresh mint. Roll tightly.
    3. Serve with tzatziki dipping sauce.
    4. **Why It Works**: Light and fresh, this dish combines the best of both cuisines.

6. Wasabi Mashed Potatoes

A bold twist on a comfort food classic.

- **Ingredients**: Potatoes, butter, milk, wasabi paste, green onions.
- **Directions**:
    1. Mash boiled potatoes with butter, milk, and a small amount of wasabi paste.
    2. Garnish with chopped green onions.
    3. **Why It Works**: The wasabi adds a surprising kick to the creamy texture of mashed potatoes.

Desserts
7. Matcha Tiramisu
A Japanese-inspired twist on the Italian classic.

- **Ingredients**: Matcha powder, ladyfingers, mascarpone cheese, sugar, cream, green tea.
- **Directions**:
    1. Soak ladyfingers in brewed green tea.
    2. Layer with a mascarpone mixture sweetened with sugar and flavored with matcha.
    3. Dust with matcha powder and chill before serving.
    4. **Why It Works**: The earthy flavor of matcha pairs beautifully with the creamy sweetness of tiramisu.

8. Churro Cannoli
A decadent dessert combining Mexican and Italian flavors.

- **Ingredients**: Cannoli shells, cinnamon-sugar mixture, cream cheese, powdered sugar, vanilla extract, chocolate chips.
- **Directions**:
    1. Roll cannoli shells in cinnamon sugar.
    2. Fill with a cream cheese mixture sweetened with powdered sugar and studded with chocolate chips.
    3. **Why It Works**: The crispy sweetness of churros meets the creamy filling of cannoli.

Drinks

9. Mango Lassi Mojito

A tropical blend of Indian and Cuban beverages.

- **Ingredients**: Mango puree, yogurt, lime juice, mint, sparkling water, rum (optional).
- **Directions**:
  1. Blend mango puree, yogurt, and lime juice. Pour over ice and top with sparkling water.
  2. Add rum for an alcoholic version and garnish with mint.
  3. **Why It Works**: The creamy richness of lassi complements the refreshing tang of mojitos.

10. Thai Spiced Hot Chocolate

A warm and aromatic drink with a Southeast Asian twist.

- **Ingredients**: Milk, cocoa powder, sugar, cinnamon, cardamom, coconut milk.
- **Directions**:
  1. Heat milk and coconut milk with cocoa powder, sugar, and spices.
  2. Serve hot with a dollop of whipped cream.
  3. **Why It Works**: The exotic spices add depth to the comforting sweetness of hot chocolate.

Setting the Scene for a Fusion Feast

1. **Highlight Origins**: Share the cultural inspiration behind each dish to create a meaningful dining experience.
2. **Pair Drinks Thoughtfully**: Choose drinks that complement the global flavors of your menu.
3. **Decor with Diversity**: Incorporate elements from the cuisines you're featuring, such as table linens or serving dishes.
4. **Encourage Curiosity**: Provide tasting notes or pairing suggestions to engage your guests in the fusion experience.

The Joy of Festive Fusion

Blending cultures through food is a beautiful way to celebrate the New Year, embracing diversity and unity in every bite. These fusion recipes offer a creative and delicious way to honor global traditions while crafting a menu that feels fresh and exciting. Whether you're hosting a dinner party or an intimate gathering, these dishes will make your New Year's celebration an unforgettable experience. Cheers to a year of discovery, connection, and exceptional flavors!

Chapter 24: Midnight Desserts: Sweets to Ring in the Year

As the clock strikes midnight, there's no better way to welcome the New Year than with an indulgent and celebratory dessert. Midnight desserts serve as the grand finale to your celebration, offering a sweet, memorable way to toast new beginnings. Whether you prefer decadent chocolate creations, sparkling treats, or globally inspired confections, this chapter is dedicated to crafting desserts that are as exciting and festive as the occasion itself.

In this chapter, you'll find a range of recipes that balance elegance, creativity, and ease of preparation. From shimmering cakes to bite-sized delights, these sweets are designed to dazzle your guests and make your New Year's celebration truly unforgettable.

Why Midnight Desserts?

1. **Symbolism**: Sweetness represents hope, joy, and good fortune for the year ahead.
2. **Celebratory Atmosphere**: Decadent desserts elevate the mood and add to the excitement of the countdown.
3. **Shared Moments**: Midnight desserts create a communal moment of indulgence, where everyone can toast to new beginnings.
4. **Visual Appeal**: Desserts offer a chance to impress guests with stunning presentations and festive touches.

Tips for Perfect Midnight Desserts

1. **Focus on Presentation**: Use edible glitter, gold leaf, or elegant platters to make desserts visually striking.
2. **Incorporate Sparkle**: Add champagne, sparkling sugar, or shimmering decorations to align with the celebratory theme.
3. **Choose Bite-Sized Options**: Offer smaller portions to allow guests to enjoy a variety of treats.
4. **Prep Ahead**: Choose desserts that can be made in advance and require minimal assembly at midnight.

Midnight Dessert Recipes

1. Champagne Cupcakes

Light and bubbly cupcakes with a hint of champagne.

- **Ingredients**: All-purpose flour, sugar, butter, eggs, champagne, baking powder, vanilla, powdered sugar.
- **Directions**:
  1. Prepare cupcake batter, replacing part of the liquid with champagne. Bake at 350°F (175°C) until golden.
  2. Make champagne frosting by mixing butter, powdered sugar, and a splash of champagne.
  3. Frost cupcakes and top with edible glitter or gold sprinkles.
  4. **Why It's Perfect**: These festive cupcakes are a sweet way to toast the New Year.

2. Midnight Chocolate Mousse

A decadent, creamy dessert that's easy to prepare ahead.

- **Ingredients**: Dark chocolate, heavy cream, sugar, eggs, vanilla extract.
- **Directions**:
  1. Melt dark chocolate and let cool slightly. Whisk eggs and sugar, then fold into chocolate.
  2. Whip cream and fold into the chocolate mixture. Portion into individual glasses and chill.
  3. Garnish with whipped cream and chocolate shavings.
  4. **Why It's Perfect**: Rich, indulgent, and perfectly portioned for midnight.

3. Golden Sparkle Truffles

Bite-sized treats coated in edible gold dust.

- **Ingredients**: Dark chocolate, heavy cream, butter, vanilla, edible gold dust.
- **Directions**:
  1. Heat cream and pour over chopped chocolate. Stir until smooth, then chill until firm.
  2. Roll into balls and coat with edible gold dust or sparkling sugar.
  3. **Why It's Perfect**: These luxurious truffles embody the glamour of New Year's Eve.

4. Sparkling Citrus Tart

A zesty dessert with a glittering finish.

- **Ingredients**: Shortbread crust, lemon curd, orange zest, sugar, edible glitter.
- **Directions**:
    1. Bake a shortbread crust and fill with lemon curd mixed with orange zest.
    2. Chill until set, then sprinkle with edible glitter for a dazzling effect.
    3. **Why It's Perfect**: Light and tangy, this dessert balances the richness of other sweets.

5. Chocolate-Covered Strawberries with Champagne Glaze

A romantic and elegant dessert that's easy to make.

- **Ingredients**: Fresh strawberries, dark chocolate, white chocolate, champagne, powdered sugar.
- **Directions**:
    1. Dip strawberries in melted dark chocolate and let set.
    2. Drizzle with white chocolate and a champagne glaze made with powdered sugar and champagne.
    3. **Why It's Perfect**: The classic combination of chocolate and fruit is elevated with a celebratory twist.

6. Midnight Macarons

Delicate French cookies filled with festive flavors.

- **Ingredients**: Almond flour, powdered sugar, egg whites, sugar, butter, champagne, food coloring.
- **Directions**:
    1. Whip egg whites and sugar into stiff peaks, then fold in almond flour and powdered sugar.
    2. Pipe into rounds and bake. Fill with champagne-flavored buttercream.
    3. Dust with edible glitter for a finishing touch.
    4. **Why It's Perfect**: Elegant and versatile, these cookies are perfect for any New Year's celebration.

7. Glimmering Chocolate Fondue

A shared dessert experience with shimmering flair.

- **Ingredients**: Dark chocolate, heavy cream, vanilla extract, edible glitter.
- **Directions**:
  1. Melt chocolate with cream and vanilla in a fondue pot.
  2. Add edible glitter and serve with fruit, marshmallows, and pound cake for dipping.
  3. **Why It's Perfect**: Interactive and festive, it encourages conversation and sharing.

8. Firecracker Popcorn

Sweet and salty popcorn with a pop of color and sparkle.

- **Ingredients**: Popcorn, white chocolate, sprinkles, edible glitter.
- **Directions**:
  1. Drizzle popcorn with melted white chocolate and toss with sprinkles and edible glitter.
  2. Let set before serving in individual cones or bowls.
  3. **Why It's Perfect**: Fun and playful, this treat is easy to enjoy while mingling.

9. Caramelized Banana Split Bites

Miniature versions of the classic dessert.

- **Ingredients**: Bananas, caramel sauce, dark chocolate, whipped cream, maraschino cherries.
- **Directions**:
  1. Slice bananas and caramelize in a pan with sugar.
  2. Assemble with chocolate drizzle, whipped cream, and cherries on toothpicks.
  3. **Why It's Perfect**: The small size makes it easy to enjoy without overindulging.

10. Layered Midnight Pavlova

A meringue dessert with layers of cream and fruit.

- **Ingredients**: Egg whites, sugar, cream, vanilla, mixed berries, edible gold stars.
- **Directions**:
  1. Whip egg whites and sugar into stiff peaks, then bake into meringue layers.
  2. Layer with whipped cream and berries. Garnish with edible gold stars.
  3. **Why It's Perfect**: Light and airy, this dessert is visually stunning and celebratory.

Decorating Tips for Midnight Desserts

1. **Add Sparkle**: Use edible glitter, shimmering sprinkles, or gold and silver accents to evoke the magic of midnight.
2. **Thematic Garnishes**: Incorporate New Year's-themed elements like clock face designs or numbers for the upcoming year.
3. **Elegant Serving Ware**: Use tiered trays, crystal bowls, or champagne coupes to elevate presentation.
4. **Individual Portions**: Serve desserts in small cups, glasses, or individual plates for easy enjoyment.

Creating a Midnight Dessert Bar

1. **Offer Variety**: Include a mix of rich, light, and fruity desserts to cater to different preferences.
2. **Set the Scene**: Decorate the dessert table with candles, fairy lights, and metallic accents for a glamorous look.
3. **Add Drinks**: Pair desserts with midnight drinks like champagne, coffee, or sparkling mocktails.
4. **Interactive Elements**: Include a fondue station or build-your-own dessert options for added fun.

A Sweet Start to the New Year

Midnight desserts are the perfect way to end the year on a high note and begin the next with joy and indulgence. These recipes combine elegance, creativity, and deliciousness to ensure your celebration is unforgettable. From sparkling treats to decadent bites, let your midnight dessert table dazzle your guests and create a moment worth toasting. Here's to a sweet and successful New Year!

Chapter 25: The Morning After: Comfort Foods for Recovery

The morning after New Year's Eve is all about comfort, recovery, and easing into the first day of the year. Whether you stayed up late partying, indulged a little too much, or simply want to start the New Year with cozy and nourishing foods, this chapter is your guide to creating dishes that restore and rejuvenate.

From hearty breakfasts to soothing drinks, these recipes are designed to be gentle on your body while providing the warmth, sustenance, and hydration you need. With a focus on balance and simplicity, this chapter will help you recover from the festivities and prepare to embrace the year ahead.

Why Comfort Foods for the Morning After?

1. **Recovery**: Hearty and hydrating foods help replenish nutrients and energy lost during celebrations.
2. **Simplicity**: Easy-to-make recipes reduce stress and effort in the kitchen after a late night.
3. **Comfort**: Familiar and warm dishes provide a sense of calm and satisfaction.
4. **Starting Fresh**: Nutritious options set a positive tone for the year ahead.

Tips for the Morning After

1. **Hydrate First**: Start with a glass of water or an electrolyte-rich drink to rehydrate after a night of festivities.
2. **Focus on Balance**: Combine protein, healthy fats, and carbohydrates for a meal that's satisfying and nourishing.
3. **Keep It Simple**: Opt for easy recipes that don't require too much effort or cleanup.
4. **Comfort Above All**: Choose dishes that bring you joy and make you feel good.

Comfort Food Recipes for Recovery
Hearty Breakfasts
1. Classic Breakfast Sandwich
A satisfying handheld option to start the day.

- **Ingredients**: English muffins, eggs, bacon or sausage, cheese, avocado, butter.
- **Directions**:
    1. Toast English muffins and cook eggs to your preference (fried or scrambled).
    2. Layer with cooked bacon or sausage, cheese, and sliced avocado.
    3. Assemble and serve warm.
    4. **Why It's Comforting**: The combination of protein, carbs, and healthy fats is energizing and filling.

2. Loaded Breakfast Hash
A one-pan dish packed with flavors and textures.

- **Ingredients**: Potatoes, onions, bell peppers, sausage or ham, eggs, cheese, olive oil.
- **Directions**:
    1. Sauté diced potatoes in olive oil until crispy. Add onions, bell peppers, and sausage or ham, cooking until tender.
    2. Make small wells in the mixture and crack eggs into them. Cover and cook until eggs are set.
    3. Top with cheese and serve.
    4. **Why It's Comforting**: This hearty dish is customizable and perfect for sharing.

3. Banana and Nut Butter Toast
A simple yet nourishing breakfast option.

- **Ingredients**: Whole-grain bread, banana slices, almond or peanut butter, honey, chia seeds.
- **Directions**:
    1. Toast the bread and spread with nut butter.
    2. Top with banana slices, a drizzle of honey, and a sprinkle of chia seeds.
    3. **Why It's Comforting**: The natural sugars and healthy fats provide quick energy and sustained fullness.

Hydrating Soups

4. Chicken and Rice Soup

A classic, soothing choice for recovery.

- **Ingredients**: Chicken broth, shredded chicken, cooked rice, carrots, celery, onions, garlic, parsley.
- **Directions**:
  1. Sauté garlic, onions, carrots, and celery in olive oil until softened. Add chicken broth and bring to a simmer.
  2. Stir in shredded chicken and cooked rice, then simmer for 10 minutes. Garnish with parsley.
  3. **Why It's Comforting**: Warm, hydrating, and easy on the stomach, this soup is the ultimate comfort food.

5. Miso Soup with Tofu and Seaweed

A light, restorative option inspired by Japanese cuisine.

- **Ingredients**: Miso paste, dashi broth, tofu, seaweed, green onions.
- **Directions**:
  1. Heat dashi broth and whisk in miso paste until dissolved.
  2. Add cubed tofu and rehydrated seaweed. Simmer for 5 minutes and garnish with green onions.
  3. **Why It's Comforting**: Packed with umami flavor and gentle on digestion, miso soup is deeply satisfying.

Comforting Mains
6. Creamy Mac and Cheese
A nostalgic, indulgent dish that's easy to prepare.

- **Ingredients**: Elbow pasta, butter, flour, milk, cheddar cheese, Parmesan, breadcrumbs.
- **Directions**:
  1. Cook pasta and set aside. Make a roux with butter and flour, then whisk in milk until thickened.
  2. Stir in shredded cheeses and mix with pasta. Top with breadcrumbs and bake at 375°F (190°C) until golden.
  3. **Why It's Comforting**: Rich and creamy, mac and cheese is the ultimate comfort food.

7. Shakshuka
A flavorful, one-pan egg dish with a spicy tomato base.

- **Ingredients**: Tomatoes, onions, garlic, bell peppers, eggs, paprika, cumin, olive oil, parsley.
- **Directions**:
  1. Sauté onions, garlic, and bell peppers in olive oil. Add tomatoes and spices, then simmer until thickened.
  2. Make wells in the sauce and crack eggs into them. Cover and cook until eggs are set. Garnish with parsley.
  3. **Why It's Comforting**: The bold flavors and hearty ingredients are both satisfying and energizing.

Sweet Treats

8. Overnight Oats with Berries

A make-ahead breakfast that's both nutritious and delicious.

- **Ingredients**: Rolled oats, almond milk, yogurt, honey, mixed berries, chia seeds.
- **Directions**:
    1. Combine oats, almond milk, yogurt, and honey in a jar.
    2. Refrigerate overnight and top with berries and chia seeds before serving.
    3. **Why It's Comforting**: Easy to prepare and nutrient-packed, this dish is perfect for recovery.

9. Pancakes with Maple Syrup

A classic breakfast indulgence to start the day with a smile.

- **Ingredients**: All-purpose flour, baking powder, sugar, milk, eggs, butter, maple syrup.
- **Directions**:
    1. Whisk dry ingredients, then mix in milk, eggs, and melted butter until smooth.
    2. Cook pancakes on a griddle and serve with butter and maple syrup.
    3. **Why It's Comforting**: Fluffy and sweet, pancakes are a delightful way to treat yourself.

Soothing Drinks

10. Ginger and Lemon Tea

A calming, hydrating drink to settle the stomach.

- **Ingredients**: Fresh ginger, lemon juice, honey, hot water.
- **Directions**:
    1. Steep sliced ginger in hot water for 5 minutes. Add lemon juice and honey to taste.
    2. **Why It's Comforting**: Ginger soothes digestion, while honey and lemon provide hydration and a touch of sweetness.

11. Recovery Smoothie

A nutrient-rich drink to boost energy levels.

- **Ingredients**: Banana, spinach, almond milk, Greek yogurt, chia seeds, honey.
- **Directions**:
    1. Blend all ingredients until smooth. Serve immediately.
    2. **Why It's Comforting**: This smoothie is packed with vitamins, minerals, and hydration for a quick recovery.

Creating a Cozy Morning After

1. **Set the Tone**: Create a relaxed atmosphere with soft music, cozy blankets, and a warm drink station.
2. **Offer Options**: Serve a mix of light and hearty dishes to cater to varying appetites.
3. **Encourage Hydration**: Provide water, herbal teas, and electrolyte-rich beverages alongside your dishes.
4. **Enjoy Together**: Make it a communal experience by enjoying the meal with family or friends.

The Perfect Start to a New Year

Comfort foods for the morning after are more than just nourishment—they're a way to ease into the year with warmth, care, and joy. These recipes combine simplicity, flavor, and a touch of indulgence to help you recover from the festivities and embrace the year ahead. Here's to a fresh start, one delicious bite at a time!

Appendix A: Measurement Conversions and Ingredient Substitutions

Cooking and baking often require precision, especially when dealing with recipes from different regions or accommodating dietary restrictions. This appendix serves as a comprehensive guide to measurement conversions and ingredient substitutions, ensuring your New Year's dishes are successful and adaptable. Whether you're working with metric units, adjusting for allergies, or out of a key ingredient, this resource will help you navigate the kitchen with confidence.

Measurement Conversions

Volume

Metric	US Customary Equivalent	Notes
1 milliliter (ml)	0.034 fluid ounces (fl oz)	About 20 drops of liquid.
5 milliliters	1 teaspoon (tsp)	Common in small quantities.
15 milliliters	1 tablespoon (tbsp)	Equal to 3 teaspoons.
240 milliliters	1 cup	Standard measuring cup.
1 liter (L)	4.23 cups	Used for larger liquid quantities.

Weight

Metric	US Customary Equivalent	Notes
1 gram (g)	0.035 ounces (oz)	Useful for small measurements.
100 grams	3.5 ounces	Often used for baking.
500 grams	1.1 pounds (lbs)	Common for larger quantities.
1 kilogram (kg)	2.2 pounds	Standard for meats and produce.

Temperature

Celsius (°C)	Fahrenheit (°F)	Conversion Formula
100°C	212°F	Boiling point of water.
180°C	356°F	Typical baking temperature.
200°C	392°F	Used for roasting.
Formula: °F	(°C × 9/5) + 32	Convert Celsius to Fahrenheit.

Ingredient Substitutions
Baking Substitutions
Flour

- **All-Purpose Flour Substitute**: Use 1 cup whole wheat flour for a nuttier flavor, or 1 cup gluten-free flour blend for a gluten-free option.
- **Self-Rising Flour**: Replace with 1 cup all-purpose flour + 1 1/2 teaspoons baking powder + 1/4 teaspoon salt.

Sugar

- **Granulated Sugar**: Substitute 1 cup granulated sugar with 3/4 cup honey, maple syrup, or agave nectar. Reduce liquid in the recipe by 1/4 cup.
- **Brown Sugar**: Use 1 cup white sugar + 1 tablespoon molasses.

Butter

- **Unsalted Butter**: Replace 1 cup butter with 1 cup margarine, coconut oil, or 1/2 cup applesauce (for baking).
- **Salted Butter**: Use unsalted butter and add 1/4 teaspoon salt per cup.

Eggs

- **Egg Substitute**: Replace 1 egg with:
    - 1/4 cup unsweetened applesauce.
    - 1 tablespoon ground flaxseed + 2.5 tablespoons water (let sit for 5 minutes).
    - 1/4 cup plain yogurt or mashed banana (for baked goods).

Cooking Substitutions
Dairy

- **Milk**: Replace 1 cup whole milk with 1 cup almond milk, oat milk, or soy milk. For creamier options, use 3/4 cup milk + 1/4 cup heavy cream.
- **Heavy Cream**: Use 3/4 cup milk + 1/4 cup melted butter, or 1 cup coconut cream.

Oil

- **Vegetable Oil**: Substitute with 1 cup coconut oil, melted butter, or olive oil (suitable for savory dishes).
- **Olive Oil**: Replace with avocado oil or grapeseed oil in a 1:1 ratio.

Broth

- **Chicken or Beef Broth**: Use 1 cup water + 1 teaspoon bouillon powder or 1 cup vegetable broth.

Vinegar

- **Apple Cider Vinegar**: Replace with white vinegar or lemon juice in equal amounts.

Herb and Spice Substitutions

Original Herb/Spice	Substitute	Notes
Fresh Basil	Fresh oregano, thyme, or parsley	Use half the amount of dried herbs.
Fresh Cilantro	Fresh parsley or mint	Mint adds a unique flavor twist.
Fresh Thyme	Dried thyme (use 1/3 of fresh amount)	Dried herbs are more concentrated.
Garlic Powder	1 fresh garlic clove (minced)	1/8 teaspoon powder = 1 clove.
Ground Ginger	1/2 teaspoon fresh grated ginger	Adjust for stronger flavor.

Liquid Substitutions

Original Liquid	Substitute	Notes
Buttermilk	1 cup milk + 1 tablespoon vinegar or lemon juice (let sit for 5 minutes).	Perfect for pancakes and baking.
Wine (Red or White)	1 cup broth + 1 tablespoon vinegar	Ideal for sauces and marinades.
Soy Sauce	1/4 cup tamari or coconut aminos	Suitable for gluten-free diets.

Gluten-Free Alternatives

Original Ingredient	Gluten-Free Substitute	Notes
Wheat Flour	Almond flour, rice flour, or gluten-free flour blend	Adjust liquids for texture.
Soy Sauce	Tamari or coconut aminos	Both are gluten-free options.
Breadcrumbs	Crushed gluten-free crackers or almond flour	Adds crunch without gluten.

Specialty Diet Substitutions
Vegan

- **Butter**: Replace with plant-based margarine or coconut oil.
- **Cheese**: Use vegan cheese shreds or nutritional yeast.
- **Milk**: Almond, soy, or oat milk are excellent alternatives.

Keto

- **Sugar**: Substitute with erythritol, stevia, or monk fruit sweeteners.
- **Flour**: Use almond flour or coconut flour.

Low-Sodium

- **Salt**: Replace with herbs, spices, or a squeeze of lemon juice for flavor enhancement.
- **Broth**: Use low-sodium broth or homemade broth.

Conversion Tools for Accuracy

1. **Digital Scale**: Use for precise weight measurements, especially in baking.
2. **Measuring Cups and Spoons**: Ensure accurate volume measurements for both dry and liquid ingredients.
3. **Conversion Apps**: Online calculators can quickly convert between metric and US customary units.

Practical Applications

- **Example 1**: You're baking a cake and run out of eggs. Replace each egg with a flaxseed mixture or applesauce for a seamless substitute.
- **Example 2**: A recipe calls for buttermilk, but you only have regular milk. Create buttermilk by adding vinegar to your milk and letting it sit.
- **Example 3**: The dish requires chicken broth, but you're cooking vegetarian. Use vegetable broth or a bouillon cube dissolved in water.

With these conversions and substitutions, you can confidently adapt recipes to your needs and preferences, ensuring every dish is a success. Whether you're working with limited ingredients or accommodating dietary restrictions, this guide empowers you to stay creative and resourceful in the kitchen.

Appendix B: Festive Table Setting Ideas and Party Planning Tips

A beautifully set table and well-organized party create the perfect atmosphere for a memorable New Year's celebration. Whether you're hosting an intimate dinner or a grand party, attention to detail in table settings and party planning can elevate the experience for your guests. This appendix provides inspiration and practical tips for crafting a festive ambiance that reflects the joy and excitement of the New Year.

Festive Table Setting Ideas

1. Choosing a Theme

- **Color Palette**: Stick to a cohesive color scheme, such as:
    - **Classic Gold and Silver**: Symbolizing elegance and celebration.
    - **Black and White**: Perfect for a chic, sophisticated look.
    - **Winter Wonderland**: Whites, blues, and icy accents for a frosty aesthetic.
- **Style**: Decide on a style that complements your celebration:
    - Formal elegance with fine china and crystal glasses.
    - Rustic charm with natural elements like wood and greenery.
    - Glamorous sparkle with glittering table runners and metallic accents.

2. Table Linens

- **Tablecloths**: Use a neutral base like white, black, or gray to let your centerpiece and decor shine. For more drama, choose metallic or sequined tablecloths.
- **Runners**: Add a touch of sophistication with a contrasting table runner, such as gold over black or a sparkly silver over white.
- **Napkins**: Coordinate cloth napkins with your theme. Fold them creatively, such as in the shape of fans or pockets to hold cutlery.

3. Centerpieces

- **Floral Arrangements**: Incorporate seasonal blooms like white roses, silver-painted eucalyptus, or evergreens.
- **Candles**: Use a mix of pillar candles, tea lights, or LED candles for a warm and inviting glow. Place them on mirrored trays or within glass hurricanes for added elegance.
- **Festive Accents**: Add metallic ornaments, string lights, or confetti to the centerpiece for a celebratory touch.
- **DIY Ideas**:
    - Fill clear glass vases with ornaments, beads, or fairy lights.
    - Create a "countdown clock" centerpiece using vintage clocks or clock-themed decor.

4. Place Settings

- **Chargers**: Add depth and formality to your place settings with metallic or patterned charger plates.
- **Plates**: Use layered plates (dinner, salad, and bread) for a polished look.
- **Cutlery**: Polished silver or gold cutlery enhances the festive feel.
- **Glassware**: Include a mix of water glasses, wine glasses, and champagne flutes. For a playful twist, use colored or etched glassware.
- **Name Cards**: Personalize the table with handwritten name cards or small tags tied to napkin rings.

5. Special Touches

- **Party Favors**: Place small favors like sparklers, mini bottles of champagne, or fortune cookies at each setting.
- **Countdown Elements**: Incorporate clock motifs or tiny hourglasses as decor.
- **Interactive Decor**: Add blank "resolution cards" for guests to write their New Year's goals and share them after dinner.

Party Planning Tips
1. Timing and Invitations

- **Set a Clear Schedule**: Decide on key moments, such as when dinner will be served, when the countdown begins, and when desserts are presented.
- **Invitations**: Choose a format that matches your style:
    - Digital invites via email or event apps for convenience.
    - Printed invitations for a formal touch.
- **RSVPs**: Request responses to finalize your guest count and accommodate dietary restrictions.

2. Menu Planning

- **Balance**: Create a menu that offers a mix of appetizers, mains, sides, desserts, and drinks to cater to different preferences.
- **Dietary Needs**: Provide options for vegetarian, gluten-free, or allergy-sensitive guests.
- **Prep Ahead**: Choose make-ahead dishes to minimize last-minute stress (see Chapter 20 for ideas).

3. Beverage Station

- **Mocktails and Cocktails**: Offer both alcoholic and non-alcoholic options (see Chapter 22 for recipes).
- **Self-Serve Bar**: Set up a drink station with mixers, garnishes, and glassware to encourage guests to craft their own drinks.
- **Toast Ready**: Have champagne or sparkling cider flutes ready for the midnight toast.

4. Entertainment

- **Music Playlist**: Curate a playlist with upbeat tracks for the party and softer tunes for dinner.
- **Games**: Include party games like trivia, charades, or a New Year's resolution guessing game.
- **Photo Booth**: Set up a photo booth with props like hats, masks, and "Happy New Year" signs for memorable pictures.

5. Lighting and Ambiance

- **Dim Lighting**: Use string lights, candles, or lanterns to create a cozy, festive glow.
- **Fairy Lights**: Drape fairy lights along the table, mantle, or windows for a magical touch.
- **Projection Effects**: Use a projector to display countdown clocks or festive visuals on a wall.

6. Guest Comfort

- **Seating Arrangements**: Ensure guests are seated where they can easily interact with those they know or introduce themselves to new people.
- **Warmth**: Provide blankets or outdoor heaters for celebrations that extend to a patio or garden.
- **Accessibility**: Place drinks, appetizers, and party essentials where guests can easily access them without interrupting others.

Post-Party Tips

1. **Prepare for Cleanup**: Have trash bags, recycling bins, and storage containers ready to quickly manage leftovers and used decor.
2. **Delegate Tasks**: Assign friends or family members simple roles, such as serving drinks or tidying up after dinner.
3. **Thank You Notes**: If guests bring gifts or help out, consider sending them a thoughtful thank-you note or message.

Example Festive Table Settings
Elegant Countdown Dinner

- **Theme**: Gold and Black
- **Decor**: Black tablecloth, gold chargers, gold cutlery, crystal glassware. Centerpiece of gold candles and small clocks.
- **Extras**: Name cards written in gold ink, mini champagne bottles at each setting.

Rustic Charm Brunch

- **Theme**: Winter Woodland
- **Decor**: Burlap table runner, wooden serving boards, evergreen sprigs, mason jar candles.
- **Extras**: Pinecone name card holders, plaid napkins tied with twine.

Playful New Year's Party

- **Theme**: Sparkling Celebration
- **Decor**: White tablecloth with sequined runner, metallic plates, glittery confetti. Centerpiece of balloons and fairy lights.
- **Extras**: Party hats and noisemakers at each place setting.

Final Thoughts

The right table settings and party planning can transform your New Year's celebration into a memorable and meaningful event. By focusing on thoughtful details, creating a welcoming ambiance, and planning ahead, you'll ensure your guests enjoy every moment. This appendix is your guide to turning your vision into reality, helping you start the New Year with style, joy, and connection. Cheers to a fabulous celebration!

<u>Message from the Author:</u>

I hope you enjoyed this book, I love astrology and knew there was not a book such as this out on the shelf. I love metaphysical items as well. Please check out my other books:

-Life of Government Benefits

-My life of Hell

-My life with Hydrocephalus

-Red Sky

-World Domination:Woman's rule

-World Domination:Woman's Rule 2: The War

-Life and Banishment of Apophis: book 1

-The Kidney Friendly Diet

-The Ultimate Hemp Cookbook

-Creating a Dispensary(legally)

-Cleanliness throughout life: the importance of showering from childhood to adulthood.

-Strong Roots: The Risks of Overcoddling children

-Hemp Horoscopes: Cosmic Insights and Earthly Healing

- Celestial Hemp Navigating the Zodiac: Through the Green Cosmos

-Astrological Hemp: Aligning The Stars with Earth's Ancient Herb

-The Astrological Guide to Hemp: Stars, Signs, and Sacred Leaves

-Green Growth: Innovative Marketing Strategies for your Hemp Products and Dispensary

-Cosmic Cannabis

-Astrological Munchies

-Henry The Hemp

-Zodiacal Roots: The Astrological Soul Of Hemp

- **Green Constellations: Intersection of Hemp and Zodiac**

-Hemp in The Houses: An astrological Adventure Through The Cannabis Galaxy

-Galactic Ganja Guide

Heavenly Hemp

Zodiac Leaves

Doctor Who Astrology

Cannastrology

Stellar Satvias and Cosmic Indicas

<u>Celestial Cannabis: A Zodiac Journey</u>

AstroHerbology: The Sky and The Soil: Volume 1

AstroHerbology:Celestial Cannabis:Volume 2

Cosmic Cannabis Cultivation

The Starry Guide to Herbal Harmony: Volume 1
The Starry Guide to Herbal Harmony: Cannabis Universe: Volume 2
Yugioh Astrology: Astrological Guide to Deck, Duels and more
Nightmare Mansion: Echoes of The Abyss
Nightmare Mansion 2: Legacy of Shadows
Nightmare Mansion 3: Shadows of the Forgotten
Nightmare Mansion 4: Echoes of the Damned
The Life and Banishment of Apophis: Book 2
Nightmare Mansion: Halls of Despair
<u>Healing with Herb: Cannabis and Hydrocephalus</u>
<u>Planetary Pot: Aligning with Astrological Herbs: Volume 1</u>
Fast Track to Freedom: 30 Days to Financial Independence Using AI, Assets, and Agile Hustles
<u>Cosmic Hemp Pathways</u>
How to Become Financially Free in 30 Days: 10,000 Paths to Prosperity
Zodiacal Herbage: Astrological Insights: Volume 1
Nightmare Mansion: Whispers in the Walls
The Daleks Invade Atlantis
Henry the hemp and Hydrocephalus

10X The Kidney Friendly Diet
Cannabis Universe: Adult coloring book
Hemp Astrology: The Healing Power of the Stars
Zodiacal Herbage: Astrological Insights: Cannabis Universe: Volume 2
<u>Planetary Pot: Aligning with Astrological Herbs: Cannabis Universes: Volume 2</u>
Doctor Who Meets the Replicators and SG-1: The Ultimate Battle for Survival
Nightmare Mansion: Curse of the Blood Moon
<u>The Celestial Stoner: A Guide to the Zodiac</u>
Cosmic Pleasures: Sex Toy Astrology for Every Sign
Hydrocephalus Astrology: Navigating the Stars and Healing Waters
Lapis and the Mischievous Chocolate Bar

Celestial Positions: Sexual Astrology for Every Sign
Apophis's Shadow Work Journal: : A Journey of Self-Discovery and Healing
Kinky Cosmos: Sexual Kink Astrology for Every Sign
Digital Cosmos: The Astrological Digimon Compendium
Stellar Seeds: The Cosmic Guide to Growing with Astrology
Apophis's Daily Gratitude Journal

Cat Astrology: Feline Mysteries of the Cosmos
The Cosmic Kama Sutra: An Astrological Guide to Sexual Positions

Unleash Your Potential: A Guided Journal Powered by AI Insights
Whispers of the Enchanted Grove

Cosmic Pleasures: An Astrological Guide to Sexual Kinks
369, 12 Manifestation Journal
Whisper of the nocturne journal(blank journal for writing or drawing)
The Boogey Book
Locked In Reflection: A Chastity Journey Through Locktober
Generating Wealth Quickly:
How to Generate $100,000 in 24 Hours
Star Magic: Harness the Power of the Universe
The Flatulence Chronicles: A Fart Journal for Self-Discovery
The Doctor and The Death Moth
Seize the Day: A Personal Seizure Tracking Journal
The Ultimate Boogeyman Safari: A Journey into the Boogie World and Beyond
Whispers of Samhain: 1,000 Spells of Love, Luck, and Lunar Magic: Samhain Spell Book
Apophis's guides:
Witch's Spellbook Crafting Guide for Halloween
<u>Frost & Flame: The Enchanted Yule Grimoire of 1000 Winter Spells</u>
<u>The Ultimate Boogey Goo Guide & Spooky Activities for Halloween Fun</u>
Harmony of the Scales: A Libra's Spellcraft for Balance and Beauty
The Enchanted Advent: 36 Days of Christmas Wonders

Nightmare Mansion: The Labyrinth of Screams
Harvest of Enchantment: 1,000 Spells of Gratitude, Love, and Fortune for Thanksgiving
The Boogey Chronicles: A Journal of Nightly Encounters and Shadowy Secrets
The 12 Days of Financial Freedom: A Step-by-Step Christmas Countdown to Transform Your Finances
Sigil of the Eternal Spiral Blank Journal
A Christmas Feast: Timeless Recipes for Every Meal
Holiday Stress-Free Solutions: A Survival Guide to Thriving During the Festive Season
Yu-Gi-Oh! Holiday Gifting Mastery: The Ultimate Guide for Fans and Newcomers Alike
Holiday Harmony: A Hydrocephalus Survival Guide for the Festive Season
Celestial Craft: The Witch's Almanac for 2025 – A Cosmic Guide to Manifestations, Moons, and Mystical Events
Doctor Who: The Toymaker's Winter Wonderland
Tulsa King Unveiled: A Thrilling Guide to Stallone's Mafia Masterpiece
Pendulum Craft: A Complete Guide to Crafting and Using Personalized Divination Tools
Nightmare Mansion: Santa's Eternal Eve
Starlight Noel: A Cosmic Journey through Christmas Mysteries
The Dark Architect: Unlocking the Blueprint of Existence

If you want solar for your home go here: https://www.harborsolar.live/apophisenterprises/

Get Some Tarot cards: https://www.makeplayingcards.com/sell/apophis-occult-shop

<u>Get some shirts: https://www.bonfire.com/store/apophis-shirt-emporium/</u>

<u>Instagrams:</u>
@apophis_enterprises,
@apophisbookemporium,
@apophisscardshop
Twitter: @apophisenterpr1
 Tiktok:@apophisenterprise
Youtube: @sg1fan23477, @FiresideRetreatKingdom
Hive: @sg1fan23477
CheeLee: @SG1fan23477

Podcast: Apophis Chat Zone: https://open.spotify.com/show/5zXbr-CLEV2xzCp8ybrfHsk?si=fb4d4fdbdce44dec

Newsletter: https://apophiss-newsletter-27c897.beehiiv.com/

If you want to support me or see posts of other projects that I have come over to: **buymeacof-fee.com/mpetchinskg**

I post there daily several times a day

Get your Dinowicca or Christmas themed digital products, especially Santa Raptor songs and other musics. Here: **https://sg1fan23477.gumroad.com**

Apophis Yuletide Digital has not only digital Christmas items, but it will have all things with Dinowicca as well as other Digital products.